ANSWERS TO COMMON
QUESTIONS ABOUT

Angels &
Demons

ANSWERS TO COMMON QUESTIONS ABOUT

Angels & Demons

H. Wayne House
Timothy J. Demy

Kregel
Publications

To Lynn Barnes and Ken Hillard—
Thank you for decades of friendship and encouragement.

"A friend loves at all times,
and a brother is born for adversity."
Proverbs 17:17

Contents

Part 2: Angels and Demons in Christian History and Theology 73

About This Series

The Answers to Common Questions series is designed to provide readers a brief summary and overview of individual topics and issues in Christian theology. For quick reference and ease in studying, the works are written in a question and answer format. The questions follow a logical progression so that those reading straight through a work will receive a greater appreciation for the topic and the issues involved. The volumes are thorough, though not exhaustive, and can be used as a set or as single volume studies. Each volume is fully documented and contains a recommended reading list for those who want to pursue the subject in greater detail.

The study of theology and the many issues within Christianity is an exciting and rewarding endeavor. For two thousand years, Christians have proclaimed the gospel of Jesus Christ and sought to accurately define and defend the doctrines of their faith as recorded in the Bible. In 2 Timothy 2:15, Christians are exhorted: "Be diligent to present yourself approved to God as a workman who does not need to be ashamed, accurately handling the word of truth." The goal of these books is to help you in your diligence and accuracy as you study God's Word and its influence in history and thought through the centuries.

Introduction

How much do you really know about angels and demons? They are both popular in our culture and are prevalent in Christianity, other religions, and even in post-Christian spirituality. Almost everyone has thoughts and opinions about them and the fascination with them at times seems boundless. *Time* magazine reported that a 2008 poll found that 55 percent of Americans believed that they had been protected at some point by a guardian angel.[1] Angelic visions and visitations seem to be a staple of contemporary spirituality. Some of these conjectures are emotional, some are sentimental, and many are shaped by cultural values that are rooted either in literature, music, or film. Sometimes ideas about angels are based on claims of experiences with angels.

Whether it is the angelic figure of Clarence in the Jimmy Stewart film *It's a Wonderful Life*, the popular 1990s television series *Touched by an Angel*, songs about love and angels, Christmas carols and holiday decorations, paintings of angels by the great artists, or the influence of John Milton's *Paradise Lost*, angels are part of our cultural psyche. Throughout the centuries there has been a fascination with angels—in that regard, our era is not unique. Angels are also biblical. In fact, there are at least 273 references to angels in the Bible, 108 in the Old Testament and 165 in the New Testament. And yet, every reference to angels in the Bible is incidental or secondary to some other topic. There is no straightforward presentation of angels in the Bible. Everything we know about them must be seen against the backdrop of the Bible's ancillary presentation of them. That doesn't diminish their importance but it does mean that we have to study a little more and think a little harder than in some more clearly defined areas of theology.

In theology, the study of angels eventually became an accepted and recognized field of inquiry called angelology, from the Greek word *angelos*, messenger. And the studies are taken seriously. And yet, we should also remember that angels are not the central focus of Christianity and should not become the focal point of our spiritual lives. This is to be reserved for Jesus Christ.

Everyone, it seems, likes angels, at least the good ones. We seem to be drawn to the possibility of discovering inside knowledge, secrets, and mysteries, and angelology touches on such matters. Information about angels appeals to our emotions as well as our intellect.

Many people have claimed encounters with angels, and perhaps they have had such a visitation—and perhaps, not. How can we really be sure? Belief in the presence of angels in times of distress is not something unique to our era. People have claimed assistance throughout history (and in many religions) by angel-like suprahuman beings.

In 1914, during the early days of World War I, there was a popular belief among British soldiers and on the English home front that angels fought with and protected British troops at the Battle of Mons. In fact, angelic involvement in war is quite a common theme in literature, religion, and military history.

Angels and demons, or at least spirits, are also prevalent in most of the religions of the world. In these traditions they have been worshipped, pondered, studied, portrayed, catalogued, and called upon for assistance. Sometimes they have been given names, and many times they are faceless. In Western religions, beliefs about angels usually focus on ideas about the creation of the world, the giving of divine revelation, and apocalyptic events. In Eastern religions, the presence of angels or benevolent spirits is usually more in the realm of assisting an individual, family, or community.

So what do we really know about angels? Are angels benevolent, malevolent, or ambivalent beings? What is the difference between a ghost, a ghoul, a demon, and a spirit? Are all of them real? What does the Bible teach about them and how do we separate fact from fiction when it comes to angels? How do we know what comprises a true encounter with an angel from a false encounter? How do we distinguish legend from truth and mystery from history? How do we separate sentimentality from truth? These are some of the questions and issues we want to investigate in the coming pages. Join us as we take a look at what the Bible says about angels and demons and answer some of the common questions on this fascinating subject.

PART 1

Angels, Satan, and Demons in the Bible

1. What is the origin of angels?

Angels are not eternal but, rather, were created by God as permanent beings. They had a beginning, but they do not die (Luke 20:36). The creation of angels by God is taught in the Old Testament. In Psalm 148:2–5, the psalmist declares:

> Praise Him, all His angels;
> Praise Him, all His hosts!
> Praise Him, sun and moon;
> Praise Him, all stars of light!
> Praise Him, highest heavens,
> And the waters that are above the heavens!
> Let them praise the name of the LORD,
> For He commanded and they were created.

Similarly, in Isaiah 44:24, God declares through the prophet:

> "Thus says the LORD, your Redeemer,
> and the one who formed you from the womb,
> 'I, the LORD, am the maker of all things,

> stretching out the heavens by Myself
> And spreading out the earth all alone . . .'"

At some point in time, at the spoken word of God, they came into existence.

In Colossians 1:16, the apostle Paul writes of Christ as Lord of creation bringing all that is known into existence. As the second person of the Trinity, Christ as God was the agent of angelic creation: "For by Him all things were created, *both* in the heavens and on earth, visible and invisible, whether thrones or dominions or rulers or authorities—all things have been created through Him and for Him." Paul's letter to the Christians in Colossae, in present-day Turkey, was written in part to combat the syncretism of Christian theology with pagan thought and a heresy that threatened the vitality of Christianity in the city. Part of the theological error being propagated was the worship of angels (2:18), which included the belief that angels were emanations from the true God. Connected with this concept was the belief that Jesus Christ was no more than an intermediary. These concepts denied the unique deity of Christ. Against this heretical background, Paul declared the deity of Christ, proclaiming Him the Creator God. Christ created and sustains the universe and all that is in it (John 1:3; Heb. 1:2, 10), including the angels.

It is important to remember three phrases in Colossians 1:16— "by Him . . . through Him . . . and for Him." Angels are not "free agents" in the world in either their existence or activity. They worship, serve, and glorify God, and so too, should we.

2. What is the nature of angels?

The word *angel* means "messenger"; it is a description of function rather than nature. It is what they do rather than what they are. The word *angel* comes originally from the Hebrew word *malach* meaning messenger. When the Old Testament was translated into Greek (the Septuagint), the word used for "messenger" was *angelos*. Eventually the Greek Bible was translated into Latin, known as the

Vulgate. From the Latin, the word *angel* came into English vocabulary through the fusion of Old English *engel* (with hard -*g*-) and Old French *angele*.

Angels are real but they are not physical, although, they often appear to have bodies. Hebrews 1:14 states that they are spirits. According to Matthew 8:16; Luke 8:2; 11:24, 26; and Acts 19:12, the same is true of the fallen angels (demons). They are spiritual beings created holy with a personal nature and distinct identity (Gen. 1:31; Mark 8:38; 1 Cor. 6:3; Heb. 1:14). From biblical references to angels, we learn that angels have personalities that include:

- Intelligence (2 Sam. 14:17, 20; 1 Peter 1:12)
- Emotions (Job 38:7; Luke 15:7; Heb. 12:22)
- Moral will (Rev. 22:8–9)

From the New Testament we learn that these elements of personality enable angels to:

- Communicate intelligently through speech (Matt. 28:5; Luke 1:13)
- Understand the divinity and power of Jesus (Mark 1:24, 34; 8:31)
- Have cognition and recognition (Luke 1:13–16; 8:31)
- Love and rejoice (Luke 15:10)
- Move (John 1:51)
- Desire (1 Peter 1:12)
- Worship (Heb. 1:6)
- Dispute or contend (Jude 9)
- Understand divine revelation (Rev. 10:5–6; 17:1–18)

Unlike God, angels have spatial limitations—they can only be in one place at a time. This is seen in Daniel 9:21–23 where an angel moves from one space to another. Also, John 1:51 depicts angels traveling between heaven and earth.

In their nature, angels are incorporeal and invisible. They are not made of fire or air as some have argued in past centuries. As spiritual beings angels are normally invisible (Col. 1:16) but have the ability to appear to humans as recorded throughout the Bible. Sometimes their appearances are physical, as in the announcement to Zacharias of the impending birth of John the Baptist, to Mary of the coming birth of Jesus the Messiah (cf. Luke 1:11–16, 26–29), and to the shepherds on the night of Jesus' birth (Luke 2:9–10). On other occasions, the appearance of angels comes in dreams as in the case of Joseph (Matt. 1:20; 2:13, 19). Their nature is important in relation to and interaction with humans. "Because angels are invisible, you and I are generally unaware of their activities behind the scenes. We have no way of telling just how many times angels have intervened on our behalf without our being aware of it."[1]

Angels have personalities, but they also have powers granted by God. In Psalm 103:20, we read:

> Bless the LORD, you His angels,
> Mighty in strength, who perform His word,
> Obeying the voice of His word!

And in 2 Thessalonians 1:7, we read of "mighty angels." Many times angels are also said to be holy (Job 5:1; 15:15; Ps. 89:7; Dan. 4:13, 17, 23; 8:13; Jude 14). They are remarkable beings created by God to minister to humans. This should be a great lesson and reminder to each of us of God's love for us.

3. What are the similarities and differences between angels and humans?

God created angels and humans to be different beings, and they were created at separate moments in time. Angels are not the spirits of deceased humans. Angels do not become humans, and humans do not become angels. Their distinctions remain throughout eternity. Both are created beings, finite beings, and limited beings, dependent on God for continued existence. Both are accountable to God for their actions and limited in their abilities and position (Matt. 24:36; John 16:11; 1 Cor. 6:3; Heb. 9:27). Both have full personality including intellect, will, and emotion; and both are capable of a direct relationship with God. But angels are also different from humans.

Angels have different natures and are a different order of being (Heb. 2:5–7). Angels are invisible and do not marry, procreate, or die (Matt. 22:28–30; Luke 20:36). Angels are spirit (Heb. 1:14), and they do not have bodies, ethnicity, or gender (though in their appearances to humans, they appear with both). Humans are both spirit and body (James 2:26). Angels are also greater in intelligence, strength, and swiftness (2 Peter 2:11). It is important to remember the similarities and differences, especially when considering depictions of angels in the arts, popular culture, and various religious movements. Sentimentality should never usurp Scripture!

4. What are the biblical classifications of angels?

As will be seen later in this book, Christian theologians through the centuries, as well as thinkers in other religions, have classified and categorized fallen angels (demons) and unfallen angels into numerous groupings. Fallen angels are those that fell along with Satan before the creation of Adam and possibly others who fell before the flood (Gen. 6:1–4). Unfallen angels are those who remained faithful to God during Lucifer's rebellion and serve God and His saints. What is most important for our study is to know what the biblical authors writing under the inspiration and guidance of the Holy Spirit say about angels.

God created the universe with design and order, and this is seen in the angelic realm (Col. 1:16). As part of the created order as recorded in Genesis 1, angels were created as good and holy spiritual beings (Gen. 1:31). It was after their creation that some used their freedom of choice to turn against God and rebel, dividing their numbers into "holy angels" (Luke 9:26), also known as "angels of God" (Luke 12:8; Heb. 1:6) or "chosen angels" (1 Tim. 5:21), and those who followed Satan in rebellion, called "the devil and his angels" (Matt. 25:41). Other than calling Satan (Beelzebul) the "ruler of the demons" (Matt. 12:24), the Bible does not speak of a further detailed hierarchy of fallen angels. Though the term *demons* is generally used for fallen angels during the time of Christ who are opposing Him, Ephesians 6:12 and Colossians 1:16 and 2:15 speak of categories of fallen spirits as "principalities, powers, rulers and authorities." The Bible gives some classification for holy angels and tells of varying functions, but it does not list a detailed chain of command for these spiritual beings. We can determine some order and structure, but this is not as finely tuned as we might wish. The various schemes put forth through the centuries are human interpretations rather than biblical declarations.

The Bible speaks of the "assembly of the holy ones" (Ps. 89:5) and "council of the holy ones" (Ps. 89:7). Interestingly and without further comment by the biblical writers, holy angels are given governmental classifications in heaven of "rulers and authorities in the heavenly places" (Eph. 3:10), and Satan's angels are said to be "spiritual forces of wickedness in the heavenly places" (Eph. 6:12). The angels in Ephesians 3:10 are probably fallen angels as they are in 6:12. From these verses in Ephesians, we can surmise that God and Satan have organized their respective angels into some structure. This is also seen in Paul's use of the phrase "all rule and authority and power and dominion" (Eph. 1:21; see also Rom. 8:38; Col. 1:16). Although it is difficult to discern the exact differences between the words used by the apostle Paul, the words used in Jewish texts of the day refer to good and evil angels.[2] In 2 Peter 2:10 and Jude 8, the phrase "angelic majesties" is used to designate dignity and authority of God's angels. Also, we know that during the time of Job, angels assembled before God (Job 1:6; 2:1). Additionally, we find angels in military formation and conflict in Revelation 12:7–9 during the coming tribulation after the rapture.

Archangel

Twice in the Bible, in 1 Thessalonians 4:16 and Jude 9, the term *archangel* is used, so we know there is such a classification and that the archangel is named Michael. In the first instance (1 Thess. 4:16), readers are told that the archangel will accompany Jesus Christ at the moment of the rapture. In both usages, the word is preceded by the definite article "the," so it is likely that there is only one such being. This is not certain, however, and it is also possible that the article may indicate identification of a well-known archangel rather than limiting the number to just one.[3] This is especially true in light of Daniel 10:13 where Michael is described as "one of the chief princes." Although the angel Gabriel is popularly thought of as an archangel, nowhere does the Bible give him this title. Other nonbiblical writings such as the *Book of Enoch* state that there are seven archangels, but the Bible identifies only one—Michael.

In Daniel 10:21 and 12:1, Michael (whose name means "who is like God?") appears as a special protector and guardian of the nation Israel. In Revelation 12:7, it is Michael who leads armies of angelic beings against the forces of Satan, and in Jude 9 we are told that Michael had something to do with the burial of Moses. Names and their meanings have special significance in the Bible; Michael's name shows his total devotion to God in direct opposition to Satan, who proudly declared before his heavenly rebellion and fall, "I will make myself like the Most High" (Isa. 14:14).

Chief Princes

As noted above, the term "chief princes" is used in Daniel 10:13 to refer to a specific group of angels of which the archangel Michael is the greatest. The apocryphal and nonbiblical *Book of Enoch* (9:1; 40:9) names four angels (Michael, Gabriel, Raphael, and Uriel) as heavenly beings who surround the throne of God. It also states, as noted above, that there are seven archangels (20:1–7) and names them as Uriel, Raguel, Michael, Seraqael, Gabriel,

Haniel, and Raphael, with later Judaism recording the name Phan-
uel as an alternate of Uriel.[4]

Cherubim

The first biblical reference to angels is the mention of cherubim
(Gen. 3:24). Unlike other angels who are messengers of God, cherubim are never portrayed in the Bible as delivering divine revelation
to humans.[5] Cherubim is the Hebrew plural form of cherub, a term
for high-ranking, powerful, and majestic beings (never specifically
called angels) who serve as guardians of the holiness of God, surround the throne of God, and defend it from the defilement of sin.
Before his fall, Satan was a cherub (Ezek. 28:14, 16). In the garden of
Eden, cherubim and a flaming sword guarded the tree of life (Gen.
3:24) after the fall of Adam and Eve.

After the Israelites left Egypt, a representation of two cherubim
made of gold was attached to the mercy seat on the ark of the covenant as part of the tabernacle in the wilderness (Exod. 25:16–22).
It was in the presence of these two figures that God said He would
dwell among His people (v. 22). They were also represented on the
veil that prevented entrance into the Holy of Holies (Exod. 26:31;
2 Chron. 3:14). Representations of cherubim were also used in
the decoration of Solomon's temple (1 Kings 6:23–29). In Ezekiel
1:4–15 and 10:15–20, it was cherubim that Ezekiel saw bearing the
throne-chariots of God (see also 2 Sam. 22:11 and Ps. 18:10). We
are also told that the future temple of God that will be rebuilt during the millennial reign of Jesus Christ on the earth (after the rapture and tribulation) will have representations of cherubim (Ezek.
41:18–20).

Seraphim

While cherubim are guardians of divine holiness, seraphim are
divine beings proclaiming God's holiness, praising God, and serving as agents of cleansing (Isa. 6:2, 6). The plural name seraphim
derives from a Hebrew verb that means "to burn" and Isaiah's

reference is the only reference to these angelic beings in the Bible. In Isaiah 6:6–8, the seraphim fly to Isaiah and touch his lips with a burning coal to purify him and cleanse him of sin so he is able to speak for God.

In Isaiah's vision, the seraphim are described as having six wings—two that cover their faces, two that cover their feet, and two with which they fly. With the first pair of wings, the seraphim cover their faces to protect themselves from the brilliance and holiness of God. The Bible says that no person has seen the unveiled glory of God and these spiritual beings are reminders of God's holiness (John 1:18; 1 Tim. 6:16). With the second pair of wings, the angels cover their feet, possibly in an attitude of reverence and awe at being in the presence of God (similar to Moses removing his sandals at the incident of the burning bush in Exod. 3:5).[6] The third set of wings is used by the angels to swiftly carry out the commands of God.

Living Creatures

Ezekiel 1:5–14 speaks of "four living beings" that are later identified as cherubim (10:15, 20). However, in Revelation 4:6, the apostle John records seeing in his vision four "living creatures" surrounding the throne of God. Various interpretations of these beings have been given through the centuries, some designating them as angels and some not. They are most likely either cherubim, seraphim, or similar spiritual beings who have a special function within the Apocalypse of John of administering divine justice (cf. Rev. 6 and 15).[7]

Watchers

We know some angels only by their assigned function and the task they perform. For example, Daniel 4:13 and 4:23 tell of an "angelic watcher." The word *watcher* in reference to angels is frequently used in the noncanonical *Book of Enoch*. Similarly, the apostle John writes in Revelation of seeing the "angel of the abyss"

(9:11); the angel "who has power over fire" (14:18); the "angel of the waters" (16:5); and an angel who binds Satan at the beginning of the millennium, Christ's thousand-year reign on earth (20:1–2). In each of these instances, as with the watchers, angels are known by their activities.

The angelic "watcher" is an especially fascinating reminder that all angels are, as biblical scholar Ron Rhodes writes, "celestial spectators of planet earth."[8] Four specific times, angels are said to be observers—Luke 15:10 when a sinner repents, Luke 12:8–9 when believers confess Jesus Christ, 1 Timothy 3:16 as witnesses to the life and ministry of Jesus Christ, and Revelation 14:10–11 when angels see those who will worship the Antichrist during the tribulation. They are witnesses to all of history (1 Cor. 4:9; 1 Tim. 5:21; 1 Peter 1:12). Angels witnessed the creation of Adam and Eve as well as the tragedy of their fall in the garden of Eden. Just as angels were present at the creation of the first Adam, so, too, were they present at the birth of Jesus Christ—the second Adam—and they announced to shepherds the birth of a "Savior, who is Christ the Lord" (Luke 2:11). Angels witnessed the public three-year ministry of Jesus before the crucifixion and they were present at the death of the Savior. Three days later, it was angels who announced the resurrection, and forty days later angels were present at the ascension of Jesus Christ into heaven. We know, too, that angels will accompany Jesus when He returns (Matt. 25:31) and fulfills biblical prophecy and the events of the end times. Angels also observe the order of church worship and thus give a reason for Christians to observe proper form (cf. 1 Cor. 11). Throughout history, angels have been faithful witnesses and watchers of the unfolding of God's plan for the ages and all of the created order. There are no secrets!

5. What is the habitation of angels?

When not serving as messengers of God, ministers of protection, or in other biblically designated activities, angels are in the presence of God in the heavenly realms where they are actively praising

God (Isa. 6:1–6; Eph. 3:10). According to Mark 13:32, their habitation is heaven. Similarly, in Galatians 1:8, Paul writes of "an angel from heaven" as though that is their normal residence. According to Revelation 21–22, at the end of human history, angels will reside with God and the redeemed of all ages in the new heavens and new earth.

As messengers of God, they come to earth but their home is heaven. This is understood from numerous passages such as 2 Chronicles 18:18; Daniel 7:10; Isaiah 6:1–6; Hebrews 12:22; and Revelation 5:11. Notably, in John 1:51, Jesus speaks of "the angels of God ascending and descending." The duration of their missions and ministries on earth may vary, but angels do not die and when their divine assignments are accomplished, heaven is their home.

6. How many angels are there?

The Bible does not say specifically how many angels were created, although on several occasions it does reference them in large numbers. In the Old Testament, God came to Mount Sinai from "the midst of ten thousand holy ones" (Deut. 33:2), and in Psalm 68:17, David writes that "the chariots of God are myriads, thousands upon thousands; the Lord is among them as at Sinai, in holiness."[9]

In Job 38:7, the angels are called the "sons of God" and are said to have joined in praise with the stars when the earth was created. The coupling of them with the innumerable stars is seen in Psalm 148:1–3 and also implies a vast number of heavenly hosts. These verses may have led the early Christian theologian Clement of Alexandria (ca. 150–ca. 215) to believe that there were as many angels as there were stars in the sky. During the Middle Ages, another Christian theologian and philosopher, Albert Magnus or Albert the Great (d. 1280), declared that there were 399,920,004 angels—relatively, a number not too different from the medieval Jewish mystic Kabbalist figure of 301,655,722.[10] Another medieval scholar, theologian Thomas Aquinas (ca. 1225–1274), did not give a specific number but declared in his work *Summa Theologiae* (also known as *Summa Theologica*) that angels "exist in exceeding great number, far beyond all material multitude."[11]

Based upon Matthew 18:10 and upon the assumption that every person has a guardian angel, some have suggested that there are as many angels as there are people. However large their number, and it is enormous, we know that the number is steady because Jesus says that angels do not procreate or die (Matt. 22:28–30). When Jesus was arrested in the garden of Gethsemane just before His trial and crucifixion, Peter (identified in John 18:10) tried to defend Him with force. Jesus, according to Matthew 26:53, told him to stop, declaring, "Do you think that I cannot appeal to My Father, and He will at once put at My disposal more than twelve legions of angels?" A legion was a Roman army unit of between three thousand and six thousand soldiers. (In Mark 5:15 and Luke 8:30, the number of demons said to be possessing a man asking Jesus for help was "legion.")

In Revelation 5:11, John writes of "many angels" and "myriads of myriads, and thousands of thousands." Other versions, such as the NIV, say "ten thousand times ten thousand." Similarly, the writer of Hebrews states that there are "myriads of angels" (12:22). John's use of these high numbers is not meant to be numerically explicit but to attest to the extremely high number of such beings (cf. Dan. 7:10).[12] The Greek term *myrias* from which we get myriad is normally understood as either a countless number or sometimes (in ancient literature) as ten thousand, with ten thousand being the largest single number used in Greek.[13]

What we do know from the collective witness of Scripture is that, at a minimum, there are thousands and thousands of angels (and demons). Whether they are as numerous as the stars in the sky or the people of the earth, they are very real and active in the affairs of heaven and earth.

7. Who is the "Angel of the Lord"?

There are numerous references in the Old Testament to "the Angel of Yahweh" ("angel of the LORD" in some translations) or "the angel of God" (e.g., Gen. 16:7–14; 18; 21:17–18; 22:11–18; 24:7; Exod. 3:2; Judges 2:1–4; 5:23; 6:11–24; 13:3–22; 2 Sam. 24:16; Zech. 1:12; 3:1–2; 12:8). While it is possible that these are angels with a specific commission or mission, each of these verses is usually understood to contain a theophany, literally "God appearance," and more specifically, a christophany, an appearance of the pre-incarnate Christ—Jesus Christ before His birth.[14] Such appearances were usually in the visible bodily form of a person. Scripture clearly affirms the preexistence of Christ (John 1:3; Col. 1:16–17; Heb. 1:2) and thus it should not be a surprise to us to read pre-incarnate manifestations. A collective study of these manifestations shows that the angel is identified as God (Gen. 16:13; 31:11–13; 48:15–16; Exod. 3:6), is a distinct person from God the Father (Gen. 24:7; Zech. 1:12–13), and that after the birth of Jesus Christ there are no further appearances of the Angel of Yahweh. As the Angel of Yahweh, Christ had several ministries, including acting as a messenger to various people (Gen. 16:7–14; 22:11–18; 31:11–13), guiding and protecting Israel (Exod. 14:19; 23:20; 2 Kings 19:35), serving as an instrument of judgment (1 Chron. 21:1–27), and being an agent of refreshment and nourishment (1 Kings 19:4–8). Notice the ministry as guide and protector of Israel noted above—according to Exodus 14:19, "the angel of God" accompanied the Israelites when they left Egypt, and in 1 Corinthians 10:4, Paul states that the Israelites drank from "a spiritual rock which followed them; and the rock was Christ." The New Testament confirms the identity of the Old Testament angel.

8. What is the ministry of angels?

Angels are servants of God who function primarily as divine messengers and who, in the present age, help Christians. The author of Hebrews writes in Hebrews 1:14: "Are they not all ministering spirits, sent out to render service for the sake of those who will inherit salvation?" In the present age much of the ministry of angels is for the benefit of those who are destined for eternal life in heaven because of their faith in Jesus Christ and His death on the cross for the forgiveness of sins.

Angels minister in heaven and on earth and because of their spiritual, noncorporeal nature, much of their work is not known to or seen by people. The ministry of angels benefits many varied recipients, among them God the Father, Jesus Christ, historic eras and events, believers throughout history, nations of the world, the unrighteous, and the church.[15] Sometimes the ministry of angels has a single focus or recipient, but often there is overlap of angelic ministry among these recipients. In short, their ministry permeates all of human experience and history on earth as well as in heaven.

In Relation to God

The primary ministry of angels is in relation to God, and in this ministry the worship and praise of God are paramount. In their praise of God, the angels proclaim the holiness of God. Thus, in Isaiah's vision, angels in heaven proclaimed antiphonally "Holy, Holy, Holy, is the Yahweh of hosts, the whole earth is full of His glory" (Isa. 6:3). In this passage and also in Psalm 148:1–2 and in Revelation 4:6–11, the angels praise God and proclaim His holiness. Similarly, in Hebrews 1:6 and Revelation 5:8–13, the angels worship God and rejoice in the actions of God as they did at the creation of the universe (Job 38:7).

In Relation to Jesus Christ

According to Colossians, not only did Christ, as a member of the Trinity, create the angels, but part of the purpose of their creation was to serve Christ. The apostle Paul writes: "For by Him all things were created, both in the heavens and on earth, visible and invisible, whether thrones or dominions or rulers or authorities—all things have been created by Him and for Him" (1:16). It is therefore no surprise that throughout the ministry of Jesus on earth angels were present. In fact, in relation to Christ, angels were active long before His birth.

Before the birth of Jesus. Seven hundred years before the birth of Jesus in Bethlehem, the prophet Isaiah had a vision in which he was in the presence of God's glory surrounded by seraphim, angelic beings (Isa. 6:1–5). In John's gospel, we are told that part of what Isaiah witnessed was the pre-incarnate Christ. In John 12:37–50, the disciple summarizes the public ministry of Jesus and the rejection of that ministry by the multitudes. He observes that even though Jesus performed many signs and miracles, He was not believed. Yet one reason Jesus performed miracles was to fulfill the prophecies of Isaiah. John then quotes from Isaiah 53:1 and Isaiah 6:10 and declares in verse 41: "These things Isaiah said, because he saw His glory, and he spoke of Him." John identifies the glory of Jesus as part of the divine glory that Isaiah witnessed with the seraphim surrounding the throne of God.

The annunciation of the birth of Jesus. Isaiah prophesied the birth of the Messiah centuries before the birth (Isa. 4:2; 7:14; 9:6–7; 11:1–5, 10; 32:1; 42:1–4; 49:1–7; 52:13–53:12; 61:1–3), but it was the angel Gabriel who told the young woman Mary, a virgin, that she would give birth to the Savior of the world, the long-awaited Messiah (Luke 1:26–38). An angel also told Joseph that Mary would give birth to a son named Jesus who would be a Savior to His people (Matt. 1:18–25).

The proclamation of the birth of Jesus. When Mary gave birth to Jesus in Bethlehem, an angel announced the birth to shepherds and was then joined by a heavenly chorus of angels praising God (Luke 2:8–15).

The protective warning for Jesus. After the birth of Jesus and the visitation by wise men from the East, Herod the Great (who ruled with the help of Rome from 40–4 B.C.) heard of the birth of Jesus and sought to kill Him. However, an angel appeared to Joseph in a dream, warned him of the danger, and told him to flee with his family to Egypt (Matt. 2:13–15). After the death of Herod, an angel again appeared to Joseph in a dream and told him to return to Israel (Matt. 2:19–21).

The presence during the ministry of Jesus. When Jesus began His three-year public ministry, angels came and ministered to Him after His temptation by Satan in the wilderness (Matt. 4:11). Shortly before His crucifixion, angels ministered to Jesus in some of His most trying moments in the garden of Gethsemane (Luke 22:43). When arrested by Roman soldiers, Jesus did not resist the arrest but declared that if He had wished to do so, more than twelve legions of angels would come to His defense (Matt. 26:53). A legion was approximately five thousand to six thousand soldiers during the era of the early Roman Empire, and more in the early Republic, so the number referenced here would be about sixty thousand angels. The angelic army was far more powerful than the Roman army!

The presence at the resurrection. An angel was the first being to witness the resurrection of Jesus from the dead, as that angel rolled away the stone that sealed the tomb of Jesus (Matt. 28:1–2). Angels also appeared to Mary and Mary Magdalene at the tomb announcing the resurrection (Matt. 28:1–7; Mark 16:1–8; Luke 24:1–10).

The presence at the ascension. Forty days after the resurrection, two angels were present at the ascension of Jesus into the heavens. They also spoke to the bewildered disciples, promising them that someday Jesus would return physically just as He had departed physically (Acts 1:10–11). From His first day on earth as an infant until His last day on earth as the crucified and risen Savior, angels watched and participated in the life and work of Jesus Christ.

The participation when Jesus fulfills prophecy. Angels will be present in the future when biblical prophecy is fulfilled just as they were in the past when prophecy was fulfilled.[16] The apostle Paul states that at the rapture of the church, there will be an archangel accompanying

Jesus. "For the Lord Himself will descend from heaven with a shout, with the voice of the archangel and with the trumpet of God, and the dead in Christ will rise first" (1 Thess. 4:16). Then after the tribulation, at the long-awaited second coming of Christ, angels will again accompany Christ as He descends to earth (Matt. 16:27; 25:31). Paul wrote of this event, stating that "the Lord Jesus will be revealed from heaven with His mighty angels in flaming fire" (2 Thess. 1:7). Angels will also be present when Jesus judges the wheat from the tares at the time of the second coming (Matt. 13:39–43). Throughout the centuries Christians have confessed and proclaimed the words from the Apostles' Creed, "He will come again to judge the living and the dead." When that occurs, angels will be present just as they were at the judgment of Adam and Eve in the garden of Eden.

In Relation to Historic Eras and Events

When something monumental occurs in God's divine plan for the ages, angels are present. This is true of the past, the present, and the future. Just as all truth is God's truth, so is all history God's history. God is sovereign and exercises His power according to an all-inclusive plan that He controls (Acts 15:18, Eph. 1:11; Ps. 135:6). As this plan unfolds in heaven and on earth, the angels are present, witnessing it and worshipping God. Angels were present at the creation of the earth and all that is in it (Job 38:6–7). They were present when Adam and Eve fell in the garden of Eden when tempted by Satan, a fallen angel (Gen. 3:1–24). At Mount Sinai, when the Mosaic Law was given, angels were present and participated in the mediation and transfer of the law from God to Moses (Ps. 68:17; Acts 7:53; Gal. 3:19; Heb. 2:2). As noted above, angels were active at the first coming of Jesus Christ (Matt. 1:20; 4:11) and resurrection (Matt. 28:2–7), and they will be participants at the second coming as well (Matt. 25:31; 1 Thess. 4:16). According to Luke's record of the early church in the book of Acts, angels were very active during the first years of the church and the new era of the church age (Acts 8:26; 10:3, 7; 12:11).

In Relation to Believers

Angels were active in the lives of believers in both the Old Testament and the New Testament and continue their ministry in the present. According to Hebrews 1:14, angels are sent by God to "render service for the sake of those who will inherit salvation." Their ministry to believers of all ages and eras is diverse and shows, in part, God's love for the redeemed. Throughout the Bible we read of their ministry to and interaction with believers. Theologian C. Fred Dickason identifies eight major ministries that angels have had to believers since biblical times.[17] In brief, these are:

Revealing. Angels have been used by God to give revelation to humans. Angels were involved in meditating the Law to humanity (Acts 7:53; Gal. 3:19). Angels were also used in interpreting divine visions (Dan. 7:15–27; 8:13–26; Zech. 4:1; 5:5; 6:5) and in mediating visions (Dan. 9:20–27; 10:1–12:13; Rev. 1:1; 22:6, 8). Angels also announced the birth of John the Baptist (Luke 1:11–20) and Jesus (Matt. 1:20–25; Luke 1:26–35; 2:8–12).

Guiding. Angels served as divine guides several times in the Bible, as when Joseph was told to flee to Egypt with Mary and Jesus (Matt. 1:20–21). In the book of Acts, Philip was directed by an angel (8:26–29); and Cornelius, a Roman centurion, was guided by an angel to send for Peter who was used by the Holy Spirit to instruct Cornelius regarding salvation (10:1–8; 11:13–14).

Providing. Angels were used on several occasions to provide physical sustenance and encouragement to humans, as in the case of Hagar and her son (Gen. 21:17–20), Elijah (1 Kings 19:5–7), and Jesus during His time in the wilderness (Matt. 4:11). According to Psalm 78:23–25, angels were also involved in the provision of the manna from heaven while the Israelites were in the wilderness for forty years.

Protecting. In the Old Testament there are several instances of angels protecting individuals in moments of distress. Such was the case when King Nebuchadnezzar placed Shadrach, Meshach, and Abed-nego in the fiery furnace for refusing to worship an idol (Dan. 3:20). The fourth figure seen in the fiery furnace may have been an angel or it may have been an appearance of the pre-incarnate Christ. Similarly, when Daniel was placed in the lions' den, an angel "shut the lions' mouths" (Dan. 6:22). According to 2 Kings 6:16, when a large force of Syrian soldiers was sent to capture Elisha, the prophet declared to his attendant, "Do not fear, for those who are with us are more than those who are with them." Elisha then prayed that God would show the angelic protectors to the attendant and God answered his prayer—"And the LORD opened the servant's eyes, and he saw; and behold, the mountain was full of horses and chariots of fire all around Elisha" (2 Kings 6:17).

Delivering. Sometimes angels protected individuals in the midst of trouble and other times angels geographically removed believers from trouble. In the Old Testament, this was the ministry of angels experienced by Lot (Gen. 19:15–17). According to Acts 5:17–32 and 12:5–10, on at least two occasions an angel opened the gates of a jail, freeing Peter and other apostles so they might continue preaching and evangelizing. Combining the ministries of protecting and delivering, in Psalm 34:7, David praised God, declaring, "The angel of the LORD encamps around those who fear Him, and rescues them." Similarly, in Psalm 91:11–12, the psalmist tells of the protection of God mediated by angels, "For He will give His angels charge concerning you, to guard you in all your ways. They will bear you up in their hands, that you do not strike your foot against a stone."

Encouraging and strengthening. In addition to physical protection and deliverance, angels served as agents of encouragement to the apostles, exhorting them to continue their ministry after being imprisoned (Acts 5:19–20).

Participating in the answer of prayer. It is God who answers prayer, but angels are sometimes used in the answering of the prayer. This was the case when Daniel prayed for the restoration of his nation in captivity (Dan. 9:20–24; 10:10–12). Certainly God can and does answer prayer apart from the ministry of angels, but He also uses them in accordance with His purposes.

Caring for the righteous at the moment of death. According to 2 Corinthians 5:8, at the moment of death, the souls of Christians are immediately in the presence of God. Angels may have some role in this instantaneous transformation. We know that, at least, prior to the death and resurrection of Christ, angels were involved in caring for the righteous dead. Jesus spoke of angels carrying Lazarus's spirit to Abraham's bosom, a figure of speech for the abode of God (Luke 16:22). Angelic escorts were commonly portrayed figures in Jewish and early Christian imagery.[18] Biblical precedence for such activity is found in texts such as Luke 16 and Jude 9, where we are told that the archangel Michael disputed with Satan over the body of Moses. As seen below, Michael will also be involved with the righteous dead during the tribulation.

In Relation to the Nations

In addition to ministering to individuals, angels are also used by God with respect to the nations. Whether or not this is a perpetual participation or only at certain divinely appointed times, we cannot be certain. But without question, there are some times of angelic activity in the affairs of nations.

Israel. Throughout the period of the exodus from Egypt, Israel was guided and watched over by an angel—or the pre-incarnate Christ in the representation of an angel (Exod. 23:20; 32:34; 33:2; Num.

20:16). The Bible also says that the archangel Michael is a special guardian of the nation Israel (Dan. 10:13, 21; 12:1) and will be active with Israel during the events of the seven-year tribulation following the rapture (Dan. 12:1–3; Rev. 12:7).

Other nations. According to Daniel 4:17 and 4:23, angels watch the nations and rulers of the world and also participate in the affairs of nations, at least those who are at times involved with biblical Israel (Dan. 10:21; 11:1). In Revelation chapters 8–9 and 16, angels are involved in the divine judgments upon the nations during the tribulation as biblical prophecy is fulfilled.

In Relation to the Unrighteous

Christians are not the only ones who are recipients of the work of angels. They also minister to those who are not Christians.

Aiding the process of evangelism. On a least two occasions recorded in the New Testament, angels were part of the process of evangelism and the conversion of unbelievers (Acts 8:26; 10:1–8).

Announcing divine judgment. We usually think of angels as the bearers of good news as they were at the birth of Jesus. However, the Bible says that, at times, they are also used by God to announce divine judgment (Gen. 19:13; Rev. 14:6–7).

Executing divine judgment. On occasion God uses angels not only as messengers of judgment but also as agents of judgment. An example of this is found in Acts 12:23 when God used an angel to strike down the ruler of Roman Israel, Herod Agrippa, who died in A.D. 44. During the seven-year tribulation, angels will be used to initiate the seven bowl judgments of Revelation 16.

Separating the righteous from the unrighteous. When Jesus Christ returns for the second coming at the end of the tribulation, there will be a separation of the living righteous from the unrighteous before Christ commences His millennial reign, and angels will be part of the process of separating the two groups (Matt. 13:24–30, 36–43; 2 Thess. 1:7–10).

In Relation to the Church

The ministries of angels to the church are the same as their ministries to individual believers, but it is that ministry multiplied by millions (or more) through the centuries. The frequency with which God uses angels is according to His plan and will. Certainly everything that God does could be accomplished without angels, yet He continues to use them as intermediaries.

In all of the ministries noted above, it is important to remember that the angels were serving on behalf of God. They were performing God's will and not acting independently on their own initiative. In Acts 12:7–10, an angel miraculously releases Peter from chains and prison, and yet, in verses 11 and 17, Peter acknowledges that was God who delivered him through the ministry of the angel. While we want to understand the work of angels, we must not let their ministries so enthrall and preoccupy us that we miss the working of God in our own lives and the lives of others.

9. Do all angels have personal names?

Only two angels in the Bible are referred to specifically by name: Michael, the archangel, whose name means literally "Who is like God?" (Dan. 10:13, 21; 12:1; Jude 9; Rev. 12:7), and Gabriel, whose name means "man of God" (Dan. 8:16; 9:21; Luke 1:19, 26). Interestingly, even the names of these two angels demonstrate their allegiance; in all they do, angels point to God not themselves. They are not to be worshipped. Michael's name stands out especially when compared with the fallen angel Satan's boast before his fall: "I will ascend above the heights of the clouds; I will make myself like the Most High" (Isa. 14:14). Satan's bold statement stands as a reminder to us that from the very beginning, everything Satan does is a lie.

We do not know from the Bible if other angels have names or not, although other Jewish and early Christian writings give names for some angels. For example, the Christian apocryphal book of *Tobit* (3:17; 12:15) and the second- or first-century B.C. Jewish *Book of Enoch* (1:20, 22, 40; 9:1; 40:9) name also Raphael (lit. "God heals") and Uriel (lit. "God is my light"), but these are found in noncanonical books (*Tobit* is considered canonical by Roman Catholics). The *Book of Enoch* also names some of the fallen angels, among them Samyza, Araqiel, Rameel, Kokabiel, Tamiel. Although many nonbiblical Christian and Jewish writings give names to unfallen and fallen angels, biblical revelation does not go beyond Michael, Gabriel, and the fallen angel Satan. In the poetry of Psalm 147:4, we read that God "counts the number of stars; He gives names to all of them." If God does so for the stars, He may also do the same for the angels. Every angel may have a personal name, but if so, it has not been revealed to us and is known only to God (and perhaps, other angels).

10. Are angels ghosts?

Angels are created spiritual beings and are not ghosts. Angels are not humans without bodies. Ghosts in Western folklore and tradition are thought to be the disembodied souls of the deceased that are still capable of roaming the earth and manifest themselves visibly to the living. They are also known as apparitions or specters. In Christian theology, the concept of ghosts as popularly understood is rejected. There is no biblical support for disembodied souls moving about the earth or occupying specific locations either to bring comfort or fear to humans.

There are, however, two passages to consider; some appeal to these in support of the idea of ghosts—1 Samuel 28:14 and Matthew 14:26. In 1 Samuel 28, Saul encourages a medium to call upon the spirit of Samuel for guidance. She does so and Samuel appears, startling the medium (28:12). The fact that she was startled likely indicates that she did not expect to be successful and recognized this to be a work of God and not of necromancy, which is prohibited in Deuteronomy 18:10–11. In this instance, it was not the medium but God who permitted Saul an encounter with Samuel in visionary form.

In Matthew 14:26, when the disciples saw Jesus coming to them in the night on the Sea of Galilee, they thought He was a ghost. "When the disciples saw Him walking on the sea, they were terrified, and said, 'It is a ghost!' And they cried out in fear" (cf. Mark 6:49–50). In this passage, the word used is *phantasma* (phantom), which in Greek literature often carried the idea of something that was unreal or an illusion. The passage does not signify the reality of ghosts but rather that the disciples believed ghosts to be a possibility, rightly or wrongly.

The idea of ghosts has been popular in literature (e.g., *Hamlet*) and Western culture for many centuries, but these ideas are not rooted in the biblical text. For the redeemed, Scripture teaches that at the moment of death, the soul is in the presence of God (2 Cor. 5:6–8; Heb. 12:23).

11. Do angels have gender?

Because angels are spirits, they do not have sexual identity, although they appear as males in biblical texts (with the exception of Zech. 5:9, where an entire scene of the passage occurs in the feminine). The two names given to angels in the Bible are masculine names—Michael, literally "who is like God?" (Dan. 10:13, 21; 12:1; Jude 9; Rev. 12:7) and Gabriel (Dan. 8:16; 9:21; Luke 1:19, 26), literally "man of God." While this name would appear to support gender, as created spiritual beings gender is outside of the nature of angels. The same can also be said of the use of the masculine pronoun in reference to angels (cf. Mark 16:5–6; Luke 24:4). Is it possible that there is more to angels than we know, including something beyond our capacity for understanding gender? Yes, but the Bible does not speak to such matters. It is interesting to note that so often in cultural portrayals of angels they are female, whereas in all biblical appearances, they are male.

12. What interaction did Jesus have with angels?

In the past, angels were involved with the life and ministry of Jesus, as they will be in the future. The Bible records the angelic ministry and presence:

At the Birth of Jesus
- Angels predicted the birth of Jesus, announcing it to both Joseph and Mary (Matt. 1:20–21; Luke 1:26–28). In the angelic announcement to Joseph in a dream, the angel is unnamed but in the announcement to Mary, it is the angel Gabriel.
- Angels announced the birth of Jesus to shepherds near Bethlehem, identifying the infant as a "Savior, who is Christ the Lord" and identifying the infant for them (Luke 2:8–15).

After the Birth of Jesus
- An angel appeared to Joseph in a dream while Jesus was an infant, warning Joseph to take his family to Egypt to escape Herod, who wanted to kill Jesus (Matt. 2:13–15). Later, after Herod's death, an angel again appeared in a dream to Joseph directing him to return with his family to their homeland (Matt. 2:19–21).

During the Ministry of Jesus
- Angels ministered to Jesus after Satan's temptations in the wilderness (Matt. 4:11).   •   Angels ministered to Jesus in the garden of Gethsemane before the arrest, trial, and crucifixion (Luke 22:43).
- Angels were prepared to defend and protect Jesus if called upon during His arrest (Matt. 26:53).

After the Resurrection of Jesus
- An angel rolled the stone away from Jesus' tomb (Matt. 28:1–2).

- Angels appeared to the women at the tomb instructing them to announce His resurrection (Matt. 28:5–6; Luke 24:5–7).

At and After the Ascension of Jesus
- Angels were present at the ascension of Jesus and spoke and comforted the bewildered disciples and predicted Christ's return (Acts 1:10–11).
- Angels were subject to Jesus during His earthly mission, just as they had also been subject to Him before the incarnation (Eph. 1:20–21; 1 Peter 3:22).

At the Second Coming of Jesus
- An angel will herald the rapture prior to the tribulation and second coming (1 Thess. 4:16).
- Angels will accompany Christ at the second coming (Matt. 25:31; 2 Thess. 1:7).
- Angels will praise and worship Christ at the second coming (Heb. 1:6).
- Angels will gather the people from all nations for judgment by Christ (Matt. 25:31–40).
- An angel will assist with the binding of Satan at the beginning of the millennium (Rev. 20:1).

From these and other verses, it is clear that angels have had and continue to have a significant role in the life and ministry of Jesus Christ and that their worship of Christ will continue through all eternity. What is remarkable for us is that the same angels that ministered to Christ minister also to us.

13. What are the biblical names of Satan?

The Bible uses many names to refer to the fallen angel Satan. The name Satan (adversary) comes from Job 1:6, "Now there was a day when the sons of God came to present themselves before the LORD, and Satan also came among them" (see also 1 Chron. 21:1; Zech. 3:1;

Matt. 4:10; Luke 10:18). The name Lucifer is derived from Isaiah 14:12. In this passage God declares:

> "How you have fallen from heaven,
> O star of the morning, son of the dawn!
> You have been cut down to the earth,
> You who have weakened the nations!"

The phrase "star of the morning" comes from the Latin word *lucifer* used in the Vulgate translation of the Hebrew word *helel*, meaning "shining one" but often translated as referring to the morning star. In this verse "star of the morning" is also a reference to the morning star, the planet Venus.

In biblical literature, names and titles frequently indicate attributes and characteristics of the individual named. This is certainly true of Satan, and there are many names and titles used for him. The list is long and thorough, including:

- Abbadon[19] (Rev. 9:11)
- Accuser of our brethren (Rev. 12:10)
- Adversary (1 Peter 5:8)
- Angel of the abyss (Rev. 9:11)
- Apollyon[20] (Rev. 9:11)
- Beelzebul[21] (Matt. 12:24; Mark 3:22; Luke 11:15)
- Belial (2 Cor. 6:15)
- Deceiving spirit (1 Kings 22:22)
- Devil[22] (Matt. 4:1; Luke 4:2; Rev. 20:2)
- Dragon (Rev. 12:3; 20:2)
- Enemy (Matt. 13:39)
- Evil one (Matt. 13:19, 38)
- Evil spirit (1 Sam. 16:14)
- Father of lies (John 8:44)
- God of this world (2 Cor. 4:4)
- Great red dragon (Rev. 12:3)

- Liar (John 8:44)
- Murderer (John 8:44)
- Prince of the power of the air (Eph. 2:2)
- Ruler of the demons (Matt. 12:24; Mark 3:22; Luke 11:15)
- Ruler of this world (John 12:31)
- Satan (Job 1:6; Matt. 4:10)
- Serpent (Gen. 3:4, 14)
- Serpent of old (Rev. 12:9; 20:2)
- Spirit that is now working in the sons of disobedience (Eph. 2:2)
- Tempter (Matt. 4:3; 1 Thess. 3:5)

From these names and titles, there should be no doubt as to the character of Satan. Nothing he does is for the spiritual well-being of anyone. Satan hates God—Father, Son, and Holy Spirit—and you.

14. What does the Bible say about the personality of Satan?

Satan is a created being who is a fallen angel. As an angel he, like all angels, has intellect, will, and emotion. In 2 Corinthians 11:3, Paul writes of Satan's intelligence: "But I am afraid that, as the serpent deceived Eve by his craftiness, your minds will be led astray from the simplicity and purity of devotion to Christ." Here we see the cunning nature of Satan. He is very smart and he is deceptive.

In Luke 22:31–32, Jesus says to Simon Peter, "Simon, Simon, behold, Satan has demanded permission to sift you like wheat; but I have prayed for you, that your faith may not fail; and you, when once you have turned again, strengthen your brothers." Satan has a strong will and is demanding. He has definite goals in this world and strives to achieve them in any way possible.

Revelation 12:17 speaks of Satan's emotions, specifically, his anger: "So the dragon was enraged with the woman, and went off to make war with the rest of her children, who keep the commandments of God and hold to the testimony of Jesus." He has an explosive personality and his anger has far-reaching consequences. Additionally, we can see aspects of his personality from some of the names and titles given to him. Jesus says of him, "He was a murderer from the beginning, and does not stand in the truth because there is no truth in him. Whenever he speaks a lie, he speaks from his own nature, for he is a liar and the father of lies" (John 8:44). Satan's pride and ambition brought spiritual death to the angels who followed him, and his actions in the garden of Eden were instrumental in bringing spiritual and physical death to all of creation throughout human history. Jesus also says that Satan is a liar. In his deeds and his words, he is the destroyer of truth, a perpetual adversary, deceiver of the world, and an opponent of the righteous (1 Peter 5:8; Rev. 12:9–10).

15. What is the nature of Satan?

Satan is not a god; he is a created spirit being with limitations (Ezek. 28:11–19. He was created as the finest of the angels with unique privileges and responsibilities. But he used these to glorify himself rather than God. He is an opponent of God but not God's equal in any way. He is not omniscient, omnipresent, or omnipotent. Even though he is powerful in his fallen state, he has limitations. God has already judged Satan, who will be held accountable by God in the future as the judgment is carried out according to God's prophetic plan (Matt. 25:41; John 16:11; Rev. 20:10). Satan cannot act without the permission of God (Job 1:12). Satan is strong, but he can be resisted (James 4:7).

Satan's nature as a spiritual being is also seen in Ezekiel 28:14, where he is said to be a cherub. As with all fallen and unfallen angels, he may appear in many forms to humans, but his essence is spirit (cf. 2 Cor. 4:4; Eph. 2:2). Everything that Satan does is a counterfeit: "Satan disguises himself as an angel of light" (2 Cor. 11:14).

16. When was Satan created?

Satan is not self-existent; he is a created being, not a deity. Satan was a created cherub and one of the highest among the angels. Although he has enormous power and is temporarily unrestrained in the world, he is still under the rule of God and will one day be judged and condemned for eternity. The Bible does not tell us when Satan was created. The Bible teaches that all of creation was made good and therefore Satan's original state as an angel was part of that creation. All angels, including Satan, were created as holy beings (Mark 8:38), by God through Christ (John 1:3; Col. 1:16–17), before the creation of the earth (Job 38:7), and by decree (Ps. 148:2, 5).

Although there is no time reference given, many biblical interpreters understand Ezekiel 28:11–19 as a reference to the creation of Satan. If so, then his creation must have been prior to the garden of Eden (Gen. 2:8) of which Ezekiel speaks (28:13).[23]

17. Is Satan omniscient?

Like all of the angels, unfallen and fallen, Satan is a being created by God through Jesus Christ the Eternal Son (John 1:3; Col. 1:16–17). He was created with great intelligence and privilege (Ezek. 28:11–19), and he was the highest of the angelic beings (28:12), but he was not created with unlimited power or as one who is all-knowing in intellect. He does not have omnipotence or omniscience. That he lacks omniscience is seen in Matthew 24:36, where Jesus speaks of the second coming: "but of that day and hour no one knows, not even the angels of heaven, nor the Son,[24] but the Father alone" (cf. Mark 13:32).

Satan's great sin was the ambitious pride of desiring to be like God (Isa. 14:12–14), and in much that he does he imitates the power and actions of God, but he cannot equal or surpass them. His power and position in creation are unique but not unlimited. Satan is not equal to God and he does not act outside of the control and plan of God. Satan is a celestial figure who is, in every characteristic and act, subordinate to God.

18. What is the nature and origin of Satan's sin?

Satan's sin was pride that originated from within him; he coveted for himself the glory, power, and authority that belong to God alone. The creature sought to usurp the Creator in an unholy rebellion. Isaiah 14:12–17 probably records Satan's downfall, and Ezekiel 28:11–19 certainly records it. While not all biblical commentators interpret the Isaiah passage as referring to Satan, such an interpretation does fit with other biblical passages about Satan such as Luke 10:18 and Revelation 22:16. In the previous verses of chapter 14, Isaiah is telling of a historical and prophetic taunt to the king of Babylon (4–11). But then the words intensify and we find words that do not fit any earthly king. (It is not uncommon for Hebrew poetry to present parallel events in heaven and earth, as is done, for example, in Psalm 45.) In verse 12 of Isaiah 14, God declares:

> "How you have fallen from heaven,
>   O star of the morning, son of the dawn!
>   You have been cut down to the earth,
>   You who have weakened the nations!"[25]

Then, five times in verses 13 and 14 we read the words "I will," showing ambition, defiance, and pride:

> "But you said in your heart,
>   'I will ascend to heaven;
>   I will raise my throne above the stars of God,
>   And I will sit on the mount of assembly
>   In the recesses of the north.
>   'I will ascend above the heights of the clouds;
>   I will make myself like the Most High.'
> "Nevertheless you will be thrust down to Sheol,
>   To the recesses of the pit."

It is possible that the passage does not refer to Satan but only to the Babylonian king Sennacherib (705–681 B.C.). Even so, there is later the likelihood of either an allusion to or a typological interpretation of Satan in the passage because of the words of Jesus in Luke

10:18: "And He said to them, 'I was watching Satan fall from heaven like lightning.'"[26]

In Ezekiel 28:1–19 there is also information about the fall of Satan, portrayed as an exalted king of Tyre, an ancient Phoenician city-state. The first ten verses of the chapter may speak of a human king of Tyre, but verses 11–19 are statements about a superhuman individual with actions and attributes that go far beyond those of a human king.[27] Among the information given in these passages, we learn that the king of Tyre (Satan):

- "had the seal of perfection, full of wisdom and perfect in beauty" (v. 12)
- was "in Eden, the garden of God" (v. 13)
- was "created" (v. 13)
- had glory—"Every precious stone was your covering" (v. 13)
- was called "anointed cherub," signifying leadership (v. 14)
- was "on the holy mountain of God," showing the divine presence (v. 14)
- was "blameless . . . until unrighteousness was found in you" (v. 15)
- showed self-promotion in "abundance of your trade" (v. 16)
- was "internally filled with violence" (v. 16)
- "sinned" (v. 16)
- was "cast . . . from the mountain of God" (v. 16)
- had pride—"heart was lifted up because of your beauty" (v. 17)
- showed poor judgment—"corrupted your wisdom by reason of your splendor" (v. 17)
- was "cast . . . to the ground" (v. 17)

In addition to these passages in the Old Testament, 1 Timothy 3:6 states that it was conceit (i.e., pride) that was the sin and downfall of Satan. Though he has been cast out of heaven, Satan still has access to it and uses that to accuse and slander God and humanity

(Job 1–2). One day, he will be completely banned from heaven and cast into eternal destruction (Rev. 12:7–9).

19. What are the activities of Satan?

Satan is active and diverse in his cosmic conflict with God and in his acts of spiritual warfare in the world.

In Relation to God and Christ

Since the moment of his rebellion, Satan has been in a losing conflict with God, opposing the person of God and the program of God. He wanted to be like God (Isa. 14:13–14) and when he was thwarted and cast from heaven, he continued his rebellion in the garden of Eden, attacking Adam and Eve and setting into motion perpetual conflict with God (Gen. 3:1–5). In this rebellion, Satan promotes false truth in the world through a counterfeit system of lies and distortions that deny the truths of God and seek to destroy anyone and anything that he can reach (Ps. 14:1–3; Eph. 2:2; 2 Thess. 2:8–11; 2 Tim. 3:5).

Animosity and strife between Satan and Christ was predicted as far back as the garden of Eden (Gen. 3:15) and continued throughout Christ's earthly ministry and crucifixion. At the beginning of Christ's ministry, Satan tempted Jesus (Matt. 4:1–11; Luke 4:2). During the ministry of Jesus, Satan desired to sift Peter like wheat (Luke 22:31) and entered into Judas, persuading him to betray Jesus (John 13:2, 27). The animosity between Satan and Jesus Christ that was first predicted after the sin of Adam and Eve in the garden of Eden will continue until the end of the millennium, when Satan is judged and cast into the Lake of Fire.

In Relation to the Nations of the World

According to Revelation 20:3, Satan actively deceives the nations of the world and will continue to do so until he is finally defeated. He has great influence in the world today (2 Cor. 4:4) and uses the fallen angels who followed him in rebellion to oppose God and deceive as many people as possible. This deception will culminate in the days of the tribulation (Rev. 16:13–16).

In Relation to Non-Christians

Satan attacks all people, Christian and non-Christian. His activities against unbelievers include:

- Preventing acceptance of the gospel (Luke 8:12)
- Blinding the mind of the unbeliever (2 Cor. 4:4)
- Distracting the unbeliever (1 John 2:15–17)
- Promoting false religion (1 Tim. 4:1–3; 1 John 4:1–4)

In Relation to Christians

Satan cannot take away the salvation and security of the Christian, but he can tempt, malign, and attack the Christian. Among the activities of Satan against the redeemed are:

- Tempting Christians to sin (Eph. 2:1–3; 1 Thess. 3:5)
- Tempting Christians to immorality (1 Cor. 7:5)
- Tempting Christians to lie (Acts 5:3)
- Accusing and slandering Christians (Rev. 12:10)
- Attempting to defeat Christians (Eph. 6:11–12)
- Causing persecution of Christians (Rev. 2:10)
- Fostering spiritual pride in Christians (1 Tim. 3:6)
- Hindering the ministry of Christians (1 Thess. 2:18)
- Opposing the Christian witness to the gospel of Christ (Matt. 13:38–39; Mark 4:15)
- Continually stalking Christians with the intent of destroying them (1 Peter 5:8)

In Relation to Prophecy and the Future

During the tribulation, much of Satan's work will be accomplished through the activities of the Antichrist. According to Revelation 12:7–12, at the midpoint of the tribulation, Satan will be cast out of his abode in the atmospheric heavens down to earth where he will continue his rebellion against God. This activity climaxes in the campaign of Armageddon, the defeat of the forces of Satan and the Antichrist, and the second coming of Jesus Christ. At the end of the tribulation, Satan will be bound so that he will not be active during the millennial reign of Christ.

At the end of the thousand-year reign of Christ on earth, there will be one final rebellion by Satan and his forces. As prophesied in Revelation 20, Satan will be set free and will rebel against Christ. In one final grasp for power and human allegiance, Satan will manifest his true nature (as he has done throughout all of history) and attempt to seize the throne of God (Rev. 20:7–9). According to Revelation 20:10, Satan's termination will be swift but everlasting. He will be cast into the Lake of Fire forever.

Satan's activities are persistent and perpetual. To underestimate them is to seriously disadvantage us and doubt the Word of God.

20. What is the habitation of Satan?

According to Scripture, there are six habitations or abodes of Satan. Some are past, one is present, and three are in future locations.[28] Just as you can survey a person's life by looking at his addresses throughout life, so, too, can the life of Satan be traced by his residences. Those habitations are:

- Over the throne of God or "upon the holy mountain of God" (Ezek. 28:11–15). Before Satan's fall he was with God as a cherub, covering the throne of God.
- The garden of Eden (Ezek. 28:13). Some interpreters believe this was not the same garden as Adam and Eve's but an earlier mineral garden.[29] Whether it was to that garden or the garden of Genesis 2–3 that Satan came in the serpent, the second abode was after the fall of Satan.
- The atmospheric heavens (Eph. 2:2; 6:12). This is the present abode of Satan, a created spirit. However, he has access to both

heaven and earth. In heaven he is the accuser of the redeemed (Job 1:2; 2:1; Rev. 12:10), and on earth he is the prince of the world who leads perpetual revolt against God, seeking to destroy the redeemed (Luke 4:5–7; John 12:31; 2 Cor. 4:4; 11:3, 14; 1 Peter 5:8).

- The earth (Rev. 12:7–12). In the middle of the seven-year tribulation, Satan will be cast from the atmospheric heavens and confined to the earth for the last half of the tribulation. During this time he will bring great chaos and calamity.
- The abyss (Rev. 20:1–3). At the end of the tribulation after the second coming of Christ, Satan will be bound and cast into the abyss (lit. "boundless" or "bottomless"), a place of temporary confinement, for a thousand years.[30]
- The lake of fire (Rev. 20:7–10). Satan's final habitation will be the lake of fire, where he and his demons will remain for eternity.

21. What is the relationship of Satan to the world?

Satan is integrally related to the world and much that occurs in it. He will not always have this relationship, but God has temporarily permitted this (1 John 2:17). In John 12:31 Jesus declared, "Now judgment is upon this world; now the ruler of this world will be cast out" (cf. 16:11). According to Jesus, Satan is the prince or ruler of the world. When Satan came to tempt Jesus in the wilderness after Jesus' baptism, Satan offered Jesus temporal power and authority, if Jesus would worship him. When Satan made this offer, Jesus did not dispute this ability (Matt. 4:8–9). This power is what John writes of in 1 John 5:19, declaring, "We know that we are of God, and the whole world lies in the power of the evil one."

John uses the word *cosmos* for the word translated "world." This is a frequent term in John's writings (105 of 185 occurrences in the New Testament) and, in his usage, normally means either the people who live on earth (John 3:16; 12:19) or a non-chaotic structured and orderly system that is functioning apart from God. Theologian Charles Ryrie writes of this usage, "This concept of the world as opposed to Christ is a new use that the word acquires in the New Testament in contrast to its usual one in Greek writings as referring to something attractive."[31] It is this world opposed to God of which Satan is the head. "The cosmos world is that system organized by Satan, headed by Satan, and run by Satan, which leaves God out and is a rival to Him."[32] In God's plan for the ages He permits Satan this temporary role, but will one day remove Satan from power and judge him.

This relationship between Satan and the world is also noted by the apostle Paul, who wrote to Christians in the city of Corinth that Satan "the god of this world has blinded the minds of the unbelieving, that they might not see the light of the gospel of the glory of Christ, who is the image of God" (2 Cor. 4:4). According to Ephesians 2:2, Satan is the "prince of the power of the air" and the "spirit that is now working in the sons of disobedience." Satan has power in the world and in the affairs of the world (Matt. 4:8–9; Luke 13:11, 16; Acts 10:38) and is the great deceiver of the world (Rev. 12:9; 20:3). Satan is the consummate liar and scam artist. He wants to create a world system that rivals the authority, power, and values of God. It is because of this hostility that John writes, "For all that is in the world, the lust of the flesh and the lust of the eyes and the boastful pride of life, is not from the Father, but is from the world. And the world is passing away, and also its lusts; but the one who does the will of God lives forever" (1 John 2:16–17). All that Satan does is counterfeit and an illusion. He turns biblical values upside down, enticing people to focus on self rather than God and seek the temporal rather than the eternal. It is for this reason that Christians are encouraged by James to "keep oneself unstained by the world" (James 1:27). Christians live in the world and may enjoy it, but they must be wise and balance priorities (1 Tim. 6:17).

Satan works on a micro level and a macro level in the world. He is interested in individuals as well as institutions and he is as happy to destroy a person as a nation. In the lives of individuals, Satan turns people away from the message of Jesus Christ, preventing them from accepting the truths of Christianity (Luke 8:12; 1 Cor. 1:18; 2 Cor. 4:3–4). He turns people away from true faith, but he also uses other people to preach lies and false religion (1 Tim. 4:1–3; 1 John 4:1–4). Satan cannot take away the salvation of those who are already Christians (Rom. 8:37–39), but he still pressures and tempts Christians (1 Cor. 7:5; 1 Thess. 3:5).

Satan has a grand strategy to deceive the nations of the world and its citizens into believing that his plan is better than God's plan and that true peace will come from him rather than Jesus Christ (Rev. 20:3). Part of this deception is thwarting the spread of the message of Jesus Christ (1 Thess. 2:18) as well as putting forth a false Christ, the Antichrist, during the future time period known as the tribulation, a seven-year era that occurs after the rapture of Christians (Rev. 13:2–4).[33]

Satan is powerful, but he is not omnipotent. He is active in the world fighting God, but he will not be victorious. We must not underestimate or overestimate his power and activity.

22. What is the future of Satan?

Satan functions in the world only because he is temporarily permitted to do so by God. Throughout history Satan has used deception and the offer of a counterfeit program to entice people away from God and His program. This began in Genesis 3:5 and will culminate in the future tribulation and the counterfeit kingdom he offers through the Antichrist (2 Thess. 2:9). Although Satan deceives both people and nations, this will not continue indefinitely (Rev. 20:3). His present activities are abundant, but his future defeat is certain.

Satan's activities will continue in the world during the present age, beyond the rapture, and into the coming seven-year tribulation. During the tribulation much of Satan's work will be accomplished through the activities of the Antichrist. According to

Revelation 12:7–12, at the midpoint of the tribulation, Satan will be cast out of his abode in the atmospheric heavens down to earth. Prophecy scholar Dr. Arnold Fruchtenbaum writes of this event:

> In the middle of the tribulation while war breaks out on earth between the Antichrist and the ten kings, war also breaks out in the atmospheric heavens. . . . The conflict is between the Archangel Michael and his forces and the archenemy Satan and his forces. Michael is victorious, and Satan and his cohorts are cast out of the atmospheric heavens and confined to the earth.
>
> Satan's confinement to the earth brings two results. *First:* Satan's access to heaven is removed, and he will no longer be able to stand before the Throne of God and be the accuser of the brethren. For this, there is rejoicing in heaven (vv. 10–12a). *Second:* Satan is now full of wrath (v. 12b). His anger is due to the fact that he knows his time is short, namely 3½ years. Because of Satan's wrath, it is *woe for the earth.* This is a very important point to note in the understanding of what is happening during the middle and second half of the tribulation.[34]

The relationship between the expulsion of Satan and the last half of the tribulation or great tribulation is very important, for it is at this point that the true character and intent of the Antichrist, Satan's human leader on earth, is revealed. All of this activity climaxes in the campaign of Armageddon, the defeat of the forces Satan and the Antichrist, and the second coming of Jesus Christ.

At the end of the tribulation, Satan will be bound so that he will not be active during the millennium and reign of Christ (Rev. 20:2–3). Once the thousand-year reign of Jesus Christ on earth ends, there will be one final rebellion by Satan and his forces. Satan will be loosed and will rebel against the millennial reign of Christ. John writes:

When the thousand years are completed, Satan will be released from his prison, and will come out to deceive the nations which are in the four corners of the earth, Gog and Magog, to gather them together for the war; the number of them is like the sand of the seashore. And they came up on the broad plain of the earth and surrounded the camp of the saints and the beloved city, and fire came down from heaven and devoured them. And the devil who deceived them was thrown into the lake of fire and brimstone, where the beast and the false prophet are also; and they will be tormented day and night forever and ever. (Rev. 20:7–10)

There is one last rebellion against God by Satan. In one final grasp for power and human allegiance, Satan will manifest his true nature (as he has done throughout all of history) and attempt to seize the throne of God. Dr. John Walvoord writes of this attempted *coup d'état:*

The thousand years of confinement will not change Satan's nature, and he will attempt to take the place of God and receive the worship and obedience that is due God alone. He will find a ready response on the part of those who have made a profession of following Christ in the Millennium but who now show their true colors. They will surround Jerusalem in an attempt to capture the capital city of the kingdom of David as well as of the entire world. The Scriptures report briefly, "But fire came down from heaven and devoured them."[35]

According to Revelation 20:10, Satan's termination will be swift but everlasting. He will be cast into the Lake of Fire, joining the Antichrist and the false prophet, who is the Antichrist's lieutenant (Rev. 13:11–18).

The Lake of Fire is the final form of hell from which no one ever leaves. This is why Satan is bound in the bottomless pit at the start of the millennium, because he will make one more appearance upon the stage of history before he is once and for all consigned to the Lake of Fire. The judgment of Satan is then followed by the judgment of the unbelieving dead, known as the great white throne judgment (Rev. 20:11–15).

It seems somewhat strange that Satan, once bound, would be loosed again to rebel. However, there is a purpose for it. This rebellion provides to all of the created order the supreme illustration of sin and its consequences. Satan will not change, and some humans, even when in a pristine environment, will manifest the sin nature acquired at the fall in the garden of Eden in Genesis 3.

History does not only include the human dimension of creation; it also involves the angelic. In the classic demonstration of interplay between the satanic and human, Satan makes his encore upon the stage of history by providing fallen humanity what it lacked during the millennium. One last time, Satan serves to embolden rebellious humanity into a deceived mob that wrongly believes it can prevail in a confrontation against an omnipotent God. Finally, through the agency of a recently released Satan, all unbelievers show their chosen allegiance and are, along with Satan, swiftly and finally judged by God.

23. What is the origin of demons?

Demons were originally good angels. According to Genesis 1:31, at the end of six days of creation, "God saw all that He had made, and behold, it was very good." Then in the next verse we read, "Thus the heavens and the earth were completed, and all their hosts" (2:1). Therefore, at some point prior to this time, the angels were created. According to Job 38:7, angels witnessed the creation of the world and rejoiced in it. The fall of some angels came at some point between the time of Genesis 1:31 and Genesis 3:1 when Satan disguised himself as a serpent and tempted Eve.

Demons are not the disembodied spirits of deceased people. According to Psalm 9:17, Luke 16:23, and Revelation 20:13, the unredeemed dead are confined in torment, awaiting final judgment and unable to move about the earth. (This also argues against the concept of ghosts as the spirits of the deceased; such apparitions as might occur are satanic deceptions rather than ghosts.) Nor are demons the offspring of the sexual union between humans and the "sons of God" recorded in Genesis 6:1–4. To argue such a view requires that one understand the "sons of God" as angels (a view we accept as likely) and that the offspring were not human (which we reject). It means that the offspring were destroyed in the flood of Noah and that somehow the spirits of the offspring became demons that continue to roam the earth. Finally, demons are not the disembodied spirits of a pre-Adamic race that was destroyed before the creation account of Genesis 1. This is a view that was argued by some Christians in the early twentieth century, but there is no textual support for such an idea in the Bible, just as there is no support for demons being disembodied spirits—something this view also requires.

Demons are fallen angels who are not eternal but were created by God originally as holy angels and chose to rebel with Satan their leader. At the time of their rebellion and the judgment of God that removed them from His presence and holiness, they acquired the status of fallen angels, also known as demons. The term *demon* is based on the Greek word *daimon*, referring to either a benevolent or malevolent spirit between the gods and humans. The New Testament authors use it only in the negative sense.

24. What are the classifications of demons?

In looking at categories of demons, one must first decide if fallen angels and demons are always identical, or if only some fallen angels become demons. While the Bible nowhere specifically says that fallen angels are demons, the biblical descriptions and activities of the two are such that theologians have consistently understood the two as identical. In Matthew 25:41, Jesus refers to the final judgment of "the devil and his angels." This clearly links fallen angels with Satan, and we believe that the totality of other biblical verses gives a portrait of fallen angels and demons as synonymous so that the terms "fallen angels" and "demons" may be used interchangeably. If, however, there is some distinction between the two, then we would argue that fallen angels that are not demons are confined awaiting final judgment (2 Peter 2:4; Jude 6) and that those fallen angels that are demons remain active in the world but will also be judged in the future. However, in our understanding of Scripture, fallen angels and demons are identical.

There are two types of these fallen spiritual beings—confined and unconfined. The unconfined are active today doing the work of Satan, and the confined are not, although some will be active briefly in the future. Thus, of the confined, some are temporarily confined and others permanently confined. We know this from the book of Revelation. Revelation 9:1–15 speaks of the fifth trumpet judgment that occurs during the first half of the seven-year tribulation. During this judgment demonic beings are portrayed as locusts and for five months bring destruction on the earth. They have been temporarily confined in hell (though still a long confinement) and are released for a brief period. Based upon these verses (which speak of temporarily confined demons) and 2 Peter 2:4 and Jude 6 (alluding to permanently confined demons), we can see two categories of "confined demons"—temporary and permanent. This category is also inferred from Luke 8:31. In the future, some are released briefly and some are not. We know that not all confined demons are released because of the wording in 2 Peter 2:4, "committed them to pits of darkness, reserved for judgment" and in Jude 6, "eternal bonds." These may not have fallen with Satan at the beginning but did so after lusting for women (Gen. 6:1f). They are given different punishment, being currently restricted, whereas the other fallen angels have access to the world now until the final judgment.

To this category of "confined demons," there are those demons who have been active from the time of their fall until the present, and who will remain active until their judgment (Eph. 6:11–12). These we call unconfined demons. Such fallen angels are unbound, have been temporarily unrestrained since their fall, and are free to carry out Satan's warfare against God and the redeemed on earth. They will be judged when Satan is judged (Rev. 20:10).

Some evangelical theologians do not make a distinction between confined and unconfined demons. They believe that 2 Peter 2:4 and Jude 6 refer to all demons and that there is no group of demons now permanently confined. In this view, all demons are assigned to hell as a permanent habitation, but they are all equally capable of leaving and acting today.[36] Either position is understandable from the Bible and both portray active demonic warfare in the world today.

25. What is the nature of demons?

Demons (fallen angels) are created spiritual beings that rebelled against God at the same time Satan rebelled. Some continue that rebellion actively in the world today, while others remain bound. They are real beings, but they are not limitless. As created beings they do not share the attributes of omniscience, omnipresence, and omnipotence with God. Demons are spirit beings; they do not have physical bodies (Eph. 6:12).

They were originally no different from those angels that did not rebel and thus have the same attributes as unfallen angels. They chose to follow Satan and give him their allegiance rather than worshipping their creator God. That they willfully followed Satan shows that they had freedom of choice and the intellect to make such a decision. Their status as angels changed when they rebelled. They were created good, as everything God made, but in pride, like Satan, they chose to defy God.

According to Mark 1:24, demons have intelligence. A demon possessing a man cried out to Jesus, "What business do we have with each other, Jesus of Nazareth? Have You come to destroy us?

I know who You are—the Holy One of God!" This verse shows recognition and intelligence. In Matthew 8:29 demons possessing two men asked Jesus, "What business do we have with each other, Son of God? Have You come here to torment us before the time?" In asking these questions, the demons showed intellectual abilities and a knowledge that one day God will judge them. Throughout their long existence, fallen angels have witnessed much history—far more than any human being. This compounds their ability to serve Satan, giving them literally thousands of years of experience in spiritual warfare against God. In Mark 5:9, when Jesus encountered a demon-possessed man, the demons identified themselves as "Legion; for we are many." They used a military term of the Roman army, commonly understood (a military unit of about six thousand in the time of the New Testament). Demons are battle-hardened veterans of cosmic conflict and to deny their potential is to misunderstand the Bible with detrimental and devastating consequences.

Paul writes in 1 Timothy 4:1 of the ability of demons to promote false doctrine that "in later times some will fall away from the faith, paying attention to deceitful spirits and doctrines of demons." This shows that their intellectual abilities can be of a high order. Demons are not simple spirits. Similarly, according to James 2:19, demons have awareness and knowledge of God and even belief in God's nature. James writes: "You believe that God is one. You do well; the demons also believe, and shudder." This verse shows that in addition to intellect, demons also have emotions.

Demons are powerful but not omnipotent. There are limits to their power. Like Satan, they can only do that which God temporarily permits (Job 1:12; 2:6). Yet, they can at times display strength beyond that of humans (Mark 5:3).

26. What are the activities of demons?

As participants with Satan in the cosmic rebellion against God, demons continue their spiritual warfare. Demons attack both Christians and non-Christians (though in different ways and with different capabilities). They, too, oppose the plan of God. Among their many activities, demons:

- May cause some mental and physical illnesses (1 Sam. 16:14; Matt. 9:33; 12:22; 17:15–18; Mark 5:4–5; Luke 8:27–29; 9:37–42). That not all illnesses are demonic is seen in the distinctions made between illness and demon activity in Matthew 4:24; Mark 1:32, 34; Luke 7:21; 9:1.
- May cause perversity (Lev. 18:6–30; Deut. 18:9–14)
- Promote idolatry (Lev. 17:7; Deut. 32:17; Ps. 106:36–38; Rev. 9:20)
- Possess animals (Mark 5:13)
- Possess unbelievers (Matt. 9:32–33; 10:8; Mark 6:13)
- Promote false religion (1 John 4:1–4)
- Deny biblical truth (1 Tim. 3:16–4:3)
- Hinder answers to prayer (Dan. 10:12–20)
- Instigate jealousy and division (James 3:13–16)
- Work with Satan against Christians (Eph. 6:12; Rev. 12:7–12)

The Christian has the permanent indwelling of the Holy Spirit (1 Cor. 6:19), and we do not believe that Christians can be possessed by demons. They may be oppressed by them outwardly but not possessed inwardly. Colossians 1:13 states that God has removed Christians from the domain of Satan: "For He rescued us from the domain of darkness, and transferred us to the kingdom of His beloved Son."

27. What is the habitation of demons?

According to 2 Peter 2:4, some fallen angels are permanently "cast into hell [lit. Tartarus]" and "committed . . . to pits of darkness." In Hellenistic and Jewish literature, Tartarus was considered a place lower than Hades. To this geographic description, Jude 6 adds that they are "kept in eternal bonds under darkness for the judgment of the great day." Thus, some are confined in hell ("bottomless pit") awaiting final judgment. We know also though that some will be temporarily released during the future tribulation (Rev. 9:1–15). Other fallen angels (demons) are active in the world today opposing the plan of God (Eph. 6:11–12). Though the specificity of their habitation is not stated in the Bible, it is reasonable to infer that these fallen angels reside with Satan. If so, then when not roaming on earth on missions from Satan, including possessing people and creatures (Mark 9:14–29), they are in the atmospheric heavens with him (Eph. 2:2; 6:12).

28. What interaction did Jesus have with Satan and demons?

Satan and demons actively attacked Jesus, His ministry, and the people around Him. Yet, in every instance Jesus was victorious. In 1 John 3:7–8, John declares: "Little children, make sure no one deceives you; the one who practices righteousness is righteous, just as He is righteous; the one who practices sin is of the devil; for the devil has sinned from the beginning. The Son of God appeared for this purpose, to destroy the works of the devil." While on earth Jesus Christ continued the long war against Satan that was first predicted in Genesis 3:15 and will be concluded at the end of the millennium (Rev. 20:10).

At the beginning of Christ's earthly ministry, Satan came and tempted Christ many times (Matt. 4:1–11), and Jesus subsequently confronted demons and the attacks of Satan throughout His ministry (Matt. 8:16; Mark 1:32; Luke 4:41). According to John 13:2, 27, Satan entered Judas, persuading him to betray Jesus.

The New Testament records nine specific instances of Jesus combating demons:

- Matthew 8:28–34 (Mark 5:1–17; Luke 8:26–37)
- Matthew 9:32–34
- Matthew 12:22–29
- Matthew 17:14–20 (Mark 9:14–28; Luke 9:37–42)

- Mark 1:21–28 (Luke 4:31–37)
- Mark 7:25–30
- Luke 8:2
- Luke 11:14
- Luke 13:10–16

Jesus also gave authority to the twelve apostles to cast out demons (Matt. 10:1, 7–8; Luke 10:17, 20). And when Judas betrayed Jesus, Judas had come under the influence and control of Satan. Judas was still responsible for his actions but there was satanic influence (Luke 22:3; cf. John 13:27).

29. What is the meaning of "tongues of angels" (1 Cor. 13:1)?

In 1 Corinthians 13:1, Paul writes: "If I speak with the tongues of men and of angels, but do not have love, I have become a noisy gong or a clanging cymbal." Some ancient and contemporary writers and proponents of mysticism and esoteric knowledge have argued that Paul is declaring that there is a unique language of angels, a heavenly language that is unknown and incomprehensible to humans. To argue this idea, 1 Corinthians 13:1 is sometimes coupled with 2 Corinthians 12:4, where Paul writes of being caught up into paradise and hearing "inexpressible words, which a man is not permitted to speak."

In the world of the first century, with a strong Roman presence and a history of Greek influence, there was an admiration for eloquence and oratory. This probably explains in part the fascination of the Corinthians with the phenomenon of *glossolalia*—speaking in tongues (which we understand to be known languages). In 1 Corinthians 13:1, Paul is speaking of his rhetorical abilities and stating that even if he used every imaginable mode of speech but doesn't have love, then his words are empty chatter and clatter. His reference to angelic language is a hyperbole, a figure of speech, similar to the other hyperboles that immediately follow this statement in the biblical text, namely, knowing all mysteries and knowledge, having all faith, having given all his possessions to the poor, and having surrendered his body to be burned. He is not saying that angels have a unique language. Nor do his words in 2 Corinthians 12:4 support the idea of an angelic language. His comment there is stating that he was forbidden to speak what he heard. As noted above, there were discussions in early Christianity (as well as in Judaism) about the potential for an angelic language that were based in part on 1 Corinthians 13:1 and noncanonical writings. In these musings it was some diversity of thought and belief that an angelic language did exist and was the same as whatever was the first human language, Hebrew, or some esoteric heavenly language.[37] Although it is an interesting idea, there is nothing in the biblical text that supports an angelic language. We know that when angels spoke to individuals in the Bible, those people were able to understand them, and it is reasonable to conclude that the angels communicated in the language of the person. We also know that there is and will be praise of God in heaven by the angels (Ps. 148:2), but there is no indication of heavenly language.

30. Are fallen angels referred to as "sons of God" in Genesis 6?

Genesis 6:2–4 is a remarkable snapshot of ancient human history and a passage that is debated with regard to its interpretation. We read in the verses:

> The sons of God saw that the daughters of men were beautiful; and they took wives for themselves, whomever they chose.
>
> Then the LORD said, "My Spirit shall not strive with man forever, because he also is flesh; nevertheless his days shall be one hundred and twenty years."
>
> The Nephilim were on the earth in those days, and also afterward, when the sons of God came in to the daughters

of men, and they bore children to them. Those were the mighty men who were of old, men of renown.

The verses come in the larger context of God's grief over the widespread human wickedness that led to the flood of Noah (Gen. 6:1–13). The depth and breadth of human rebellion against God was so great that the human race was destroyed except for the remnant of Noah's family in the ark. This section is a contrast in the fate of the pre-flood world and the fate of Noah; the former receiving judgment and the latter, grace. Part of the pre-flood corruption is the incident of the marrying and union of the "sons of God" with the "daughters of men" in verse 2.

In the Bible, the Hebrew phrase translated "sons of God" can mean either people (Deut. 14:1; 32:5; Ps. 73:15; Hos. 1:10) or angels (Job 1:6; 2:1, 38:7; Pss. 29:1; 89:6).[38] The phrase occurs twice in Genesis 6:2–4 and how it is interpreted affects the understanding of the identity of the "Nephilim" in 6:4 (a word used again only in Num. 13:33, where it clearly refers to humans).

The "sons of God" are likely either despotic rulers controlled or indwelt by fallen angels, or fallen angels in human bodies.[39] Our interpretation is that they are indeed fallen angels. If the "sons of God" are understood as angels (as has been the prevailing view through the centuries), then they are among the group of fallen angels that followed Satan in his rebellion against God (Isa. 14:12–20; Ezek. 28:16–19; Jude 6).

Like Satan, these angels overstepped their bounds by seizing that which was not theirs—human wives. Likewise, some humans (though we don't know how many), in an act reminiscent of Adam and Eve partaking of the forbidden fruit (Gen. 3:1–7), also overstepped their bounds and cohabitated with the angels. The angels, taking human form, tried to seize part of creation and the humans tried to seize divinity (6:2). One of the results of the union was the birth of the Nephilim, ancient heroes, who appeared on earth after the marriage (6:4). So abhorrent was this and other activities that God responded to this widespread evil by placing a limit on His protection of humanity and ultimately judging all of creation except for Noah and his family (6:5–8). (While it is true that Jesus taught in Matthew 22:30 that angels do not marry, His point was that there is no marriage in heaven. Marriage is limited to earth. He was not talking about this perversion of marriage on earth.)

The passage does not tell us how widespread the practice was, but the implication from verse 1 that talks about population growth is that the sons of God took all they wished. Evil and the human family were both multiplying. The Nephilim may well be part of the source of the legends and mythology that survives to the present day. The world after the flood was very different from the one before the flood. Throughout the centuries and generations after the flood, the memory of that world became distorted and the Nephilim, mighty men and mythic figures, came to be seen as gods. They were not gods. The passage is also a polemic against the ancient pagan belief that kings and mighty warriors had divine origins. When a person fails to uphold the truths of the Bible, everything in life, including history, becomes distorted.

31. Did Jesus preach to fallen angels in 1 Peter 3:19?

In his first epistle to Christians who were undergoing persecution and suffering for their faith, Peter encourages his readers to stand firm in their faith, reminding them that it is better to suffer for doing what is right than for what is wrong (3:17). He then writes: For Christ also died for sins once for all, the just for the unjust, so that He might bring us to God, having been put to death in the flesh, but made alive in the spirit; in which also He went and made proclamation to the spirits now in prison, who once were disobedient, when the patience of God kept waiting in the

days of Noah, during the construction of the ark, in which
a few, that is, eight persons, were brought safely through the
water. (1 Peter 3:18–20)

When did Jesus preach to spirits in prison and who were they?
Peter's words about the preaching of Jesus are found in an extended
passage (3:13–4:19) on the meaning and purpose of suffering in the
lives of Christians. In these verses Peter reminds readers of the suffering of Jesus Christ in His undeserved death and the results that
came from that death. The death of Jesus was not a defeat but a
spiritual victory that brought salvation to all who believe. Through
His death and resurrection, Jesus was triumphant over sin, death,
and Satan. Moreover, nothing can come against Christians that is
beyond the power and control of Jesus Christ (3:22).

The triumph of Jesus in the crucifixion and resurrection is certain and not in question. What has been debated through the centuries is when and how Jesus made proclamation to spirits in prison.[40]

One common view is the one associated with a later form of
the Apostles' Creed (but not the longer and more detailed Nicene
Creed) in the words "he descended into hell," which understands
that between the crucifixion and resurrection Jesus preached to
imprisoned spirits in hell.[41] These spirits are understood to have
been either fallen angels, perhaps from Genesis 6, or humans from
the time of Noah or other Old Testament times, that are awaiting
the final judgment of God at the end of this age. Often this proclamation is then viewed to have been one of condemnation in which
Jesus said in effect "I told you so!" and announced His victory over
sin and death.[42] Also associated with this view, but taking a different interpretive view, is an understanding of a second chance at
salvation after death (though v. 20 limits the audience to those of
Noah's day). While this passage is often cited in support of such a
descent, we do not find the passage to teach such an activity (nor
does it teach it in Eph. 4:9). There also is not any support in the
Bible for a second chance of salvation after death (Heb. 9:27).

A second view is that Jesus proclaimed His victory to fallen angels not between His death and resurrection but at the time (unrecorded) of His ascension into heaven (Acts 1:9). There was a strong tradition and belief within Judaism during the New Testament era of fallen angels being kept in prison (see, for example, the nonbiblical *Book of Enoch* 10–16, 21).

A third major view with a long history of support (including Augustine, Aquinas, and many during the Reformation) is that the pre-incarnate Christ preached through Noah to his generation. In this understanding, the preaching was done by Christ through the Holy Spirit and the person of Noah. Just as the Holy Spirit spoke through King David in his day (Acts 1:16; 4:25), so too, did it happen in Noah's day while he was building the ark before the great flood. The message that was preached was one of repentance to the unbelievers of Noah's generation who refused to repent and are now in hell. The view also fits well with 1 Peter 1:11, which speaks of the pre-incarnate Christ speaking through the Old Testament prophets. One shortcoming of this view is that "spirit" is almost never used in the New Testament in reference to people. None of the interpretations is fully satisfactory and each has grammatical, lexical, or theological shortfalls, though the third view seems most consistent with the immediate context.

What is certain is that Jesus' resurrection was confirmation of all that was prophesied in the Old Testament and that Jesus Christ "is at the right hand of God, having gone into heaven, after angels and authorities and powers had been subjected to Him" (3:22).

32. Who are the angels in Jude 6–7?

Jude's letter was written to warn Christians against false teaching and to exhort them to stand firm in their faith. In verses 6 and 7, he writes:

> And angels who did not keep their own domain, but abandoned their proper abode, He has kept in eternal bonds

under darkness for the judgment of the great day, just as Sodom and Gomorrah and the cities around them, since they in the same way as these indulged in gross immorality and went after strange flesh, are exhibited as an example in undergoing the punishment of eternal fire.

These verses are a reference to the fallen angels of Genesis 6:1–4. Their sin was one of sexual immorality in cohabiting with human women.[43] Jude states that these fallen angels have been kept in bondage since their sin, awaiting final judgment. They have not been capable of serving Satan as demons in the world as have the other angels that fell from heaven when they rebelled against God.[44] Jude is reminding readers that all sin will be judged (Matt. 25:41; Rev. 20:10).

33. Where does the Bible say that the archangel Michael argued with Satan as Jude 9 states?

Apart from Satan, the Bible mentions only two angels by name, Gabriel and Michael. According to Daniel 12:1, Michael is a special guardian of the affairs of the nation Israel. And in Revelation 12:7, we are told that Michael and the angels will one day wage war against Satan and his fallen angels, likely at the midpoint of the tribulation. Only in Jude 9 is recorded the unusual confrontation between Michael and Satan over the body of Moses.[45] Jude declares: "But Michael the archangel, when he disputed with the devil and argued about the body of Moses, did not dare pronounce against him a railing judgment, but said, 'The Lord rebuke you!"

The death of Moses is recorded in Deuteronomy 34:1–6, but there is no mention of Satan and Michael struggling over his body. We are simply told that he died on Mount Pisgah and his burial place is unknown. While there were many Jewish traditions about the death of Moses, the Bible speaks very little about it. However, there was in Jude's day an apocryphal writing called *The Assumption of Moses* that tells of this conflict. Satan's argument over the body of Moses occurred because Moses killed the Egyptian overseer (Exod.

2:11–12), and Satan was arguing that Moses was a murderer. The writing *The Assumption of Moses* is not part of the Bible and is now lost except for a small portion. Although not inspired, parts of it may be valid where the contents do not contradict the Bible or biblical doctrine.

Even though Jude was writing under the guidance and inspiration of the Holy Spirit, he was not limited to the contents of the Old Testament for historical information. Details that he and other biblical authors included became part of God's inerrant Word once recorded. Biblical authors are not restricted to citing only biblical writings (cf. Paul in Acts 17 on the hill of Mars in Athens). Even though the latter writings are not inspired, they may contain true statements. There is no reason to doubt the validity of this conflict between Michael and Satan.

Jude shows great respect for celestial beings in this verse as he argues that if Michael, a mighty archangel, referred a dispute with Satan to the sovereignty of God, then how much more respect should mere false teachers show for celestial beings. The teachers were wrong in their attitudes and their doctrine.

Jude was written, in part, to warn readers about false teachers and innovators who were promoting views and doctrines that were contrary to biblical teaching. He strongly denounces these things and warns against the dangers of mixing true and false teaching. He also warns against becoming indifferent to the truths of the Bible. Some of the teachings of the false teachers involved a rejection and slandering of reality and ministry of angels. While the Bible does not teach exhaustively about angels, it does teach of their creation, nature, organization, and ministry. They are very real and important in the Bible and throughout the ages. Nothing in the Bible is insignificant or irrelevant.

34. What are "angelic measurements" (Rev. 21:17)?

In Revelation 21, John tells of his vision of the New Jerusalem that will exist after the millennial reign of Jesus Christ and after the final judgment. Surrounding the city is a large wall that is 144 cubits thick. We read:

> The one who spoke with me had a gold measuring rod to measure the city, and its gates and its wall. The city is laid out as a square, and its length is as great as the width; and he measured the city with the rod, fifteen hundred miles; its length and width and height are equal. And he measured its wall, seventy-two yards, according to human measurements, which are also angelic measurements. (vv. 15–17)

From verse 9, we know that the measurements are being taken by an angel ("Then one of the seven angels who had the seven bowls full of the seven last plagues came and spoke with me") and from verse 17 we understand the measurements are being given in human units of measurement. The phrase "angelic measurements" is simply an acknowledgment of those two facts and is saying that the angel's calculations are no different than human calculations. There is no additional angelic standard of measurement.

PART 2

Angels and Demons in Christian History and Theology

35. How were angels understood at Qumran?

The literature from the Dead Sea Scrolls manuscripts and fragments found at Qumran is extensive and diverse.[1] Among the ideas found in the scrolls are angels as keepers of wisdom and sharers in the worship of the participants in the Qumran community. There are discussions of the work of fallen ("angels of destruction") and unfallen angels. At Qumran, fragments were found of portions of the nonbiblical *Book of Enoch*, a writing that is partially contemporaneous with the Qumran community, but it is not clear how well the book was received by the community.[2] Regarding the role of angels at Qumran, R. M. M. Tuschling writes that angelology had two functions at Qumran:

> Firstly, angelological ideas perform a (retrospective) apologetic function, justifying the secession from mainstream Judaism, even though they are not themselves the theological point at issue. The Qumran community belongs to the lot of the righteous, which includes angels and is headed by

73

the variously titled chief angel (Michael, Prince of Lights, etc.).

Secondly, the angels function as role models for the Qumran community.... angels are companions and models of right behaviour, e.g. ritual purity and heavenly singing. This presupposes the concept of a community between angels and human beings, strikingly visible at Qumran.[3]

Angels were part of the doctrines of the Qumran community and belief in them shaped their worship and rituals. Some of their beliefs corresponded to biblical teaching and some did not, but angelology was an important part of this unique Jewish sect and community in the area northwest of the Dead Sea.

36. How were angels portrayed in the *Book of Enoch*?

The *Book of Enoch* (also known as *1 Enoch*) is a Jewish religious work ascribed to Enoch, the great-grandfather of Noah. The dating of the book, written in more than one section, is usually considered to be between the third and first century B.C. It is not part of the canon of the Bible (though it is accepted as canonical by the Ethiopian Orthodox Church and Eritrean Orthodox Church). It was known in the Jewish and early Christian world but generally rejected as canonical and was considered what is known today as part of the Pseudepigrapha, falsely attributed works. It is, however, part of the Jewish mystical tradition and was also very influential at Qumran. Other similar writings among the Pseudepigrapha include: *Assumption of Moses*, *Book of Jubilees*, *Letter of Aristeas*, *Greek Apocalypse of Baruch*, and *Psalms of Solomon*. However, some of the church fathers, such as the author of the *Epistle of Barnabas*, Athenagoras, Clement of Alexandria, Irenaeus, and Tertullian knew of and accepted the work to varying degrees. The *Book of Enoch* is quoted in the New Testament in Jude 14–15, referring to angels as "holy ones." Jude writes: "It was also about these men that Enoch, in the seventh generation from Adam, prophesied, saying, 'Behold, the Lord came with many thousands of His holy ones, to execute judgment upon all, and to convict all the ungodly of all their ungodly deeds which they have done in an ungodly way, and of all the harsh things which ungodly sinners have spoken against Him.'" (Jude quotes the *Book of Enoch* not because the book is inspired but because what it reports is true and evidently spoken by Enoch.)

The *Book of Enoch*, or at least portions of it, were translated into Aramaic, Greek, Latin, and Ge'ez (Southern Ethiopic). Portions of the book in Aramaic have been found as part of the Dead Sea Scrolls at Qumran. Knowledge of the full content of the work was largely lost in the West until the seventeenth century, although portions of it or synopses of it were likely known and may have influenced writings such as *Beowulf* and *Paradise Lost*.[4]

Angels are called "watchers" in the *Book of Enoch*, especially in the first part, sections 1–36, known also as the "Book of Watchers." The story of the fallen angels is found in three places in the *Book of Enoch* (6–19; 67:6, 69; 86–88) and was central in the development of some of the nonbiblical views of the origins of evil and forbidden knowledge (cf. *Jubilees* 10:1–14). In the "Book of Watchers," there is a description of the fall of the angels who are said to have fathered the Nephilim of Genesis 6:1–2 as well as a discussion of twenty named angels who, it is said, were the leaders of two hundred fallen angels in their rebellion with Satan against God. There is also detailed discussion of the alleged interaction of these fallen angels (especially one named Azazel) with humans, instructing them in the weapons of war, metallurgy, and art.[5] There is also a discussion of the work of four holy angels, Michael, Gabriel (named in the Bible), Uriel, and Raphael (named in the deuterocanonical book of Tobit, considered canonical in Roman Catholicism and Eastern Orthodoxy). The portion that contains sections 83–90, known as the "Book of Dream Visions," also has an extensive angelology including a history of the destruction of the Nephilim.

The material on angels is interesting and, along with the remainder of the book's contents, gives us some insight into the cultural and religious ideas circulating in the Jewish and Christian worlds at the time of Jesus Christ. It also shows the source of some misconceptions about angels. However, the material does not provide supporting information for biblical angelology. Certainly it is not inspired, but it may explain how some of this was understood by the first-century authors, even New Testament authors, so it does provide support in interpretation.

37. How did the early Christians view angels and demons?

Angels and demons were very much a part of the beliefs of early Christianity although statements about them are often brief and without doctrinal elaboration, assuming knowledge and acceptance of the biblical text. Belief in angels and demons was normative and accepted from biblical teaching without detailed investigation. Many of the comments come from commentary of biblical accounts of angels such as at the birth of Jesus or the ascension of Jesus.

The early history of Christianity is often divided into four eras: the age of the apostles (ca. 30–100), the age of the apostolic fathers (ca. 100–150), the age of the apologists (ca. 150–300), and the age of the theologians (ca. 300–600). In each of these eras, there were comments about angels and demons, but the discussions became more detailed and nuanced as the centuries progressed and as Christianity became more prominent and less threatened by persecution.

When Christians in the early centuries of the church wrote about angels and demons, it was usually in the context of written sermons and comments on specific biblical texts. There are not extended theological treatises or discussions on angelology until the fifth and sixth centuries. It was the writing of Pseudo-Dionysius's *The Celestial Hierarchy* (*De Colesti Hierarchia*) in the fifth century that presented the first treatise dedicated solely to the subject of angels in Christian literature. There were, however, portions of other writings that dealt with angels such as *De principiis* (1.8), a short doctrinal work written by Origen prior to 231. Angels are also discussed in Augustine's *The City of God* (*De Civitate Dei*), especially Books 9 and 10. One thing that emerges is that some church fathers' statements may be orthodox on one doctrine and aberrant or heretical on another. Or they may be orthodox on one aspect of a doctrine and heretical on another aspect. Such is the case of the second-century author of the work *Shepherd of Hermas*, considered one of the apostolic fathers. The *Shepherd*, likely based on misunderstanding Old Testament references to "the angel of the Lord," wrongly portrays Jesus as an angel.[6] So too, did Origen, as he speculated that Satan and the demons would, in the future, be fully restored. In arguing this, he wrongly believed that he was within the bounds of orthodox speculation. His view on this was condemned in the sixth century as teaching universal salvation.[7] Other views by Origen rejected by orthodox Christianity are his apparent beliefs that angels can become human beings and human beings can become angels.[8]

Among the many doctrines of Christianity, it was Christology that was the primary focus of the early Christians. By necessity, the person and work of Jesus Christ was the core of patristic interest and endeavor. In an environment where Christians were often persecuted and killed because of their faith, it was essential to define and articulate what they believed about Jesus the Messiah as both God and human.

The doctrine of angels in the early centuries of Christianity was not only a continuation of views held during the biblical era but also an interaction with philosophical systems such as Neo-Platonism, occult religions, and the deities of Roman and Greek paganism. Often what one finds in the early Christian writings are statements of distinction and differentiation from nonbiblical views without great detail or comment. There is frequently simply the quoting of or reference to biblical texts.

In general, the Fathers held that angels and demons were created spiritual beings with immaterial bodies of an uncertain nature made by God either before the events of Genesis 1 or at the time of Genesis 1:4 when light was separated from darkness. Angels are not minor deities and in accordance with Colossians 2:18, and against Gnosticism, they are not to be worshipped.[9] They were created with reason and freedom for making personal choices, and for those who fell, their fall (excluding Satan) was either through pride (Augustine, John Chrysostom, Tatian, Gregory the Great) or sexual sin as recorded in the events of Genesis 6:2-4 (Justin Martyr, Clement of Alexandria, Ireneaus, Tertullian, Cyprian) or both (Athenagoras).[10]

Based upon the Septuagint (Greek translation of the Old Testament) reading of Deuteronomy 32:8 that translated the last portion of the verse "according to the number of the sons of Israel" as "according to the number of the angels of God," many of the Fathers believed that each nation was assigned an angel to guide it, provide protection and temporal assistance, and encourage each nation toward Christianity.[11] This, then, became important in evangelism in the multicultural and religious world of early Christianity. "No matter how perverted they are, they retain some vestige of the natural revelation, and that vestige is due to the angels who have passed it on to them and who strive to keep it alive among them."[12] At the same time, it was argued by some such as Clement of Alexandria (150-ca. 215) that fallen angels were responsible for the perversion of the truths of God and they were the source of philosophy.[13]

Early Christian angelology set boundaries on speculation regarding angels. For instance, that angels were created beings was orthodoxy, but the timing of their creation by God was not firmly established and was open to discussion.[14] Matters such as this were formalized in the Nicene Creed, first formulated at the Council of Nicea in 325 and rearticulated and reaffirmed at the Council of Chalcedon in 451 with the words "We believe in one God, the

Father Almighty, maker of heaven and earth, of all that is, seen and unseen."

It is clear that the Fathers believed that angels were part of the life of nations and large groups of people; they also believed that guardian angels were part of the lives of individuals, as were demons. They based this on their interpretations of Genesis 48:16, Matthew 18:10, and Acts 12:15.[15] And some Fathers held that each individual had a specific angel and demon that were in conflict.[16] This latter view was also upheld in the medieval era, and it is probably from this idea that we sometimes see in art and popular culture portrayals of an angel on one shoulder of a person and a demon on the other. Ideas never arise in a vacuum!

38. What is the history of the Christian hierarchy of angels?

While the Bible gives classifications of angels, there is no explicit reference to a structural hierarchy of angels in the Bible apart from the mention of the archangel in 1 Thessalonians 4:16 and Jude 9. Functions, roles, ministries, and types such as cherubim and seraphim are given, but not a chain-of-command structure. The systematized and detailed development of an angelic hierarchy came later in the history of angelology.

The most detailed and influential work on an angelic hierarchy was written in Greek by an individual noted earlier who wrote under the pseudonym Dionysius the Areopagite (named after Dionysius the Areopagite, the Athenian convert of Paul in Acts 17:34), known today as Pseudo-Dionysius. His work *The Celestial Hierarchy*, along with three other treatises and ten letters, was translated into Syriac and Latin and became very influential in Christianity in the East and the West.

The works of Pseudo-Dionysius were strongly influenced by Neoplatonism in both concept and terminology, blending philosophy and theology. Yet, in the Christological controversies of the fifth century, both the orthodox Christians who assented to the creed and theology of the Council of Chalcedon (451) and the dissenting Monophysite theologians accepted the writings as legitimate. The authenticity and legitimacy of the writings was accepted in the East and West, even by the Protestant Reformers, until the early seventeenth century.[17]

The Celestial Hierarchy was especially prominent in the Latin West and used by Thomas Aquinas (1225–1274) in the *Summa theologica* (Part I, Q. 108 citing *Hierarchia* 6.7–9). According to this structure that drew on Ephesians 1:21 ("rule and authority and power and dominion") and Colossians 1:16 ("thrones or dominions or rulers or authorities"), there were three spheres or "choirs" of angels in the hierarchy, each with three orders:

- First Order—Seraphim, Cherubim, Thrones (all equal in rank)
- Second Order—Authorities (Dominions), Lordships (Virtues), Powers
- Third Order—Principalities, Archangels, Angels[18]

Though not the only hierarchy proposed throughout the centuries, the scheme of Pseudo-Dionysius became the most widely accepted. Other hierarchies did not always have the same number of choirs and the numbers varied from seven to nine to eleven. Among the many schemes are those of:

- Clement of Rome (first century)—eleven choirs
- Ambrose (fourth century)—nine choirs   •   J e r o m e (fourth century)—seven choirs
- Gregory the Great (sixth century)—nine choirs
- Isidore of Seville (seventh century)—nine choirs
- John of Damascus (eighth century)—nine choirs
- Hildegard of Bingen (twelfth century)—nine choirs
- Thomas Aquinas (thirteenth century)—nine choirs
- Dante Alighieri (fourteenth century)—nine choirs

Interestingly, Augustine (354–430), one of the most influential theologians in church history, identified seven groups of angels but did not expand on their hierarchy as did Pseudo-Dionysius.[19] However, it was the Italian poet Dante Alighieri's *Divine Comedy*, the classic epic poem, that popularized the concept of the nine choirs of angels for most people. Dante divided the angels into nine choirs, almost exactly the same as Pseudo-Dionysius (seraphim, cherubim, thrones, dominations, virtues, powers, principalities, archangels, angels).

39. What did the medieval theologians say about angels and demons?

Angels were the subject of extensive study in the medieval world (though never the major focus of theology), and many of the ideas about angels that are found in the history of the doctrine of angels emerged in the medieval era. Although the early church fathers wrote of angels, it was after the fifth century that angelology began to develop as a distinct area of theology. Much of this can be attributed to the work *The Celestial Hierarchy*. By the time of Thomas Aquinas (1225–1274) and Bonaventure (ca. 1217–1274) more than five hundred years later, angels were firmly part of the study of theology and extensive writing about them was to be found in many theology books. Medieval historian David Keck writes of angels and medieval culture:

> Angels permeated the physical, temporal, and intellectual landscape of the medieval West. Sculptures, stained glass, coins, clerical vestments, and pilgrim's badges all bore images of the celestial spirits. . . . By the thirteenth century, angelology had become a required, formal part of the theological curriculum at the University of Paris, and Bonaventure, Aquinas, and their fellow scholastics were required to develop complex angelological systems.[20]

As noted above, it was the writings of Dominican theologian Thomas Aquinas and Franciscan theologian Bonaventure that were most influential in medieval angelology—Aquinas through his massive theology *Summa theologica* and Bonaventure through his *Commentary on the Sentences of Lombard*. There was a revival in interest in the works of Pseudo-Dionysius and, when coupled with the study of the works of Aristotle that were just becoming widely known, angelology flourished. Aristotle's works "transformed the Christian understanding of angels by providing a coherent set of metaphysical concepts congenial to angelic speculation."[21] But his works also presented challenges that evoked lengthy responses:

> The arrival of rival intellectual systems in medieval Christianity thus compelled certain twelfth- and almost all thirteenth-century scholastics to explore the creation of angels with greater clarity and with more depth than their immediate theological predecessors. That philosophers had asserted the existence of angel-like beings suggested that theologians could speak of a natural angelology, and indeed, it became possible to formulate philosophical proofs demonstrating that the existence of angels was required.[22]

As medieval Christians studied angels, they also renewed study and exegesis of biblical texts, especially the creation and fall texts of Genesis along with the writings of Augustine, to bolster their inquiries.

Medieval theologians did not abandon biblical texts and earlier Christian thought on angels. Rather, they sought to answer questions about the creation and work of angels that their theological predecessors had omitted. They tried to systematize all knowledge about angels from earlier sources in conjunction with philosophical inquiry according to the methods of Scholasticism. "The Middle Ages inherited the early church's readings of the angels of the Bible, and what is perhaps most striking is the basic continuity between the two eras."[23] They attempted to be precise, methodical, and comprehensive. Just as earlier Christians had combated Gnosticism, Platonism, Neo-Platonism, paganism, and heresy with regard to angels, so did the medieval theologians. They drew on the earlier Fathers and theologians such as Augustine to combat Gnostic and Cathar dualists, pagan magicians, and philosophical ideas deemed incompatible with the Bible and orthodoxy. These angelic investigations reached a zenith in 1300. Keck observes:

> The story of the unfolding of angelology in the Middle Ages and the permeation of medieval society by angels culminates in the thirteenth century. By the year 1300, when Dante sets off on his poetic journey through the afterlife, angelic doctrines, habits, and expectations had reached their fullest expression, which later medieval centuries may continue, modify, or dismiss, but to which they do not significantly add.[24]

The study of angels was not done as an independent inquiry divorced from the remainder of theology but as an integral aspect of theology and especially of anthropology—the doctrine of humanity. In part, medieval theologians investigated angels because of their belief that angels were the closest beings in the created order to humans and their concept that the knowledge of angels would enhance a theological understanding of people. "Whereas modern scientists study the origins of the apes to uncover clues about humanity, medieval theologians investigated angels."[25]

Medieval theologians tried to be comprehensive in their study of angels. Questions regarding angelic origins, nature, purpose, form, matter, personhood, knowledge, abilities, order, goodness, sexuality, work, emotions, will, intellect, location, motion, manifestations, and destiny were all part of medieval angelology. So, too, did they study demons and Satan. In all of their work, these

Christians had a threefold purpose. First, they wanted to understand the Bible and theology in order to strengthen Christians and Christianity. Second, they wanted to be able to understand the world God created and in which they lived. Third, they wanted to defend Christianity against detractors and have a comprehensive apologetic for their faith. To do this, these thinkers used the study of the Bible and the question and answer format known to them as the *questio*, a method that had developed in the eleventh and twelfth centuries and popularized in the writings of Peter Lombard (ca. 1100–1160).[26] These inquiries were coupled with an interest in the study of nature and the probing of the properties of the created order including astronomy of which angelology was considered integral. Metaphysics, philosophical categories, and the limits of human knowledge were all part of the theological questioning of the age.[27]

Prior to the *Summa theologica* by Aquinas, the *The Four Books of Sentences* (*Libri Quattuor Sententiarum*) of Peter Lombard written around 1150 were the most influential theology text for medieval Christians. Lombard's work integrated angelology with the remainder of theology and addressed questions about angels that had been part of Christian thought through the earlier centuries.[28]

The *Celestial Hierarchy* of Pseudo-Dionysius had been the first full theological treatise on angels several centuries before the work of Lombard, but Lombard's theology presented the first systematic theology of angels in the history of Christian angelology.[29] It was upon this work that theologians such as Bonaventure and Aquinas built.

The angelology of Aquinas, very important in the history of the doctrine, is found in the *Summa theologica* in Part 1 Questions 50–64 (1.50–64) and is structured as follows:

Q. 50. Of the Substance of the Angels Absolutely Considered
Q. 51. Of the Angels in Comparison with Bodies
Q. 52. Of the Angels in Relation to Place

Q. 53. Of the Local Movement of the Angels

Q. 54. Of the Knowledge of the Angels

Q. 55. Of the Medium of the Angelic Knowledge

Q. 56. Of the Angels' Knowledge of Immaterial Things

Q. 57. Of the Angels' Knowledge of Material Things

Q. 58. Of the Mode of the Angelic Knowledge

Q. 59. The Will of the Angels

Q. 60. Of the Love or Dilection of the Angels

Q. 61. Of the Production of the Angels in the Order of Natural Being

Q. 62. Of the Perfection of the Angels in the Order of Grace and of Glory

Q. 63. The Malice of the Angels with Regard to Sin

Q. 64. The Punishment of the Demons

Each of the questions is divided into further questions with objections and lengthy answers.[30]

Aquinas speculated on the nature of the angels from the vantage point of Scholastic philosophy. He used a synthesis of philosophy and Scripture (Scholasticism) to study the nature, powers, and ordering of the angels. Based on his studies, he argued that God had given angels three primary roles—the worship of God (Ps. 148:1–2), the implementation of the will of God (Ps. 103:20), and the role as messengers of God. Additionally, angels also petition God with prayers on behalf of individuals, especially in the role of guardian angels (Matt. 18:10).

Guardian angels were also part of medieval angelology. Bonaventure believed that every individual had a guardian angel from the moment of conception. He also held that the soul was capable of being tempted before birth by demons and therefore the guardian angel's ministry was essential even while an infant was in the womb. An individual could not lose their guardian angel, and it was thought that for the unsaved the presence of the guardian angel provided a hope for salvation.[31] Based upon

interpretations of Revelation 8:3, medieval Christians firmly believed that angels were involved in the transmitting of prayers
to heaven, constituting an important link between the natural
world and the realm of the supernatural. Medieval theologians
also investigated the role of angels in prophecy and the end of
the world. Prominent in this area were the writings of Joachim of
Fiore (ca. 1135–1202).[32] Satan and demons were also very much a
part of medieval theology.[33]

Ideas such as these influenced daily spirituality and religious
practices as well as theology. Prayers for angelic protection while
on a pilgrimage or crusade were commonplace, as was the com-
memoration of angels on religious feast days, belief in the protection of guardian angels from demonic assaults, and the belief in
angels as participants in the prayers of the faithful. Angels were
an active part of the worldview of medieval laity as well as clerics.
"Angelology had become habitual and unavoidable."[34] At times this
led to excessive emphases and erroneous beliefs and practices but
rarely, if ever, was there denial of the presence and work of angels—
fallen and unfallen.

40. What did the Protestant Reformers say about angels and demons?

As with theology in the Middle Ages and earlier centuries,
angelology during the Reformation was not the primary focus of
theological discussion (or dissension). Yet, it was a doctrine that
was studied and preached. As the Reformers viewed and discussed
angelology, they did so against what they understood as a twofold
background—angelology of the medieval Scholastics embodied
in Catholic doctrine and practices and angelology of Renaissance
humanists embodied in Neo-Platonism. Separated from ecclesias-
tical, theological, and biblical investigations, Renaissance humanists studied angelology in the decades preceding the Reformation
and the Reformers argued against these views as well as earlier
Scholastic views. Historian Joad Raymond observes:

On the eve of the Reformation the greatest interest in the doctrine of angels, at least beyond the immediately practical side, was expressed by humanists interested in Neoplatonism. . . . Renaissance Neoplatonists reiterated in new contexts traditional beliefs about the government of the world by angels, and added confused interest in daemons and in cabbalistic angels' names and in Gnostic myths. . . . Protestants associated Neoplatonism with two tendencies in thinking about angels. First, a contribution to theories of angelic names and cosmic intervention. Secondly, Neoplatonism was associated with the corruption of upright religion, and thus could be polemically conflated with Catholic elaboration on angels."[35]

In the investigations of the humanists, Reformers such as John Calvin (1509–1564) saw nothing worthwhile and instructed believers to "forsake that *Platonicall* philosophie, to seeke the way to God by Angels' which was pure superstition."[36]

The sixteenth-century Protestant Reformers also reacted strongly against many practices and beliefs they believed were unbiblical within Roman Catholicism, including excessive devotion to the Virgin Mary, the cult of saints, and an inordinate speculation about angels. Peter Marshall and Alexandra Walsham note the Reformers' reactions against Catholicism:

The Protestant Reformations of the sixteenth century launched a fundamental assault upon the established economy of the sacred, denouncing such central features of late medieval doctrine and piety as the cult of the saints and intercession for the souls in purgatory as human inventions with no foundation in scripture. There was no doubting that angels had been badly compromised by their collaboration with man of the worst excesses of the late medieval devotional regime. Much in the traditional understanding

of their roles was simply unacceptable from the perspective
of reformers committed to the doctrine of justification by
faith alone, such as the offering of prayers to angels, and
their role along with the saints as mediators for humanity.[37]

The Reformers did not deny the reality and ministries of angels,
but they did not view angelology as a doctrine that required the
detailed examinations and speculations afforded it during the previous centuries. For the Reformers, angels were definitely biblical and active in the world—but they were not to be scrutinized
excessively.

Martin Luther (1483–1546) fervently upheld belief in angels,
demons, and Satan.[38] In the words to his hymn "A Mighty Fortress
Is Our God," Luther wrote of the world as "with devils filled."
Additionally, in his *Small Catechism* written for the instruction of
children, Luther wrote in the morning and evening prayers to be
recited "Let Thy holy angel be with me, that the Wicked Foe may
have no power over me." There was no doubt in Luther's mind or
theology of the existence and work of angels, elect and evil.

"Luther's expansive embrace of a wide range of teachings about
the function and importance of angels contrasts with Calvin's more
measured and minimalist approach to them as ministering spirits
and divine messengers."[39] Luther does indeed discuss angels more
frequently than Calvin, and his writings are sprinkled with comments regarding angels, whereas Calvin largely limits his discussions to Book 1 of *The Institutes of the Christian Religion*.

Luther accepts the idea of guardian angels and the doctrine of
Michael as the protecting angel of the Jews. He rejects worship of
the angels but does not think it inappropriate to call upon them
when *in extremis* (in danger of death). As a former Augustinian
monk and one recipient of Augustine's theology and heritage,
Luther understands that humans are intermediate beings between
angels and animals. Luther does not, however, involve himself with
the intricacies of angelic metaphysics or physics.[40] He also shifted in

his views on angels. In his early *Lectures on the Psalms* (1513–1515), following Franciscan angelology, he argued for a hierarchy of ten ranks of angels, but later in his *Lectures on Genesis* (1536–1546), he rejected the idea as spurious.[41] A survey of the thousands of times Luther mentions angels in his many writings shows that "the angels were important to Luther throughout his life, and they reveal moreover, that he was often far more tolerant of medieval teaching concerning these spirits than was Calvin."[42]

Luther believed that angels were examples of the Christian life because of their obedience to the will of God, but he also cautioned against looking to the angels for divine messages instead of looking to the Bible. Raymond summarizes Luther's attitude toward angels well, writing: "Luther's position on angels is much like his position on art: they have a non-essential role to play in worship, and as long as they do not become the focus of undue attention it is not impossible that contemplating them will lead the faithful man closer to true faith."[43] This was not the same view as that of John Calvin or the English Reformers. For the latter especially, the iconography of angels was especially problematic and something to be shunned and, at times, destroyed.[44]

Indeed, Protestants were not unanimous in their views of the limits of angelic presence and protection—especially regarding the doctrine of a particular guardian angel being assigned to a person at birth. Luther fully supported the idea, but later second-generation Reformers feared that upholding such a belief might lead to excessive devotion to angels. John Calvin never came to a final determination, stating, "But whether individual angels have been assigned to individual believers for their protection, I dare not affirm with confidence."[45] Yet, these differences among Protestants were not polarizing differences that occurred along confessional lines or created dissension among Protestants. They were differences of emphasis and interpretation, but without the animosity, contention, and conflict that was found in other areas of theology (such as in the meaning of the Lord's Supper). Other Reformers such as

Philipp Melanchthon (1497–1560) and Heinrich Bullinger (1504–1575), John Knox (ca. 1513–1572), and Huldrych Zwingli (1484–1531) also commented on angels, but none to the extent of Luther and Calvin. Throughout all the writings of these theologians, there was a presupposition of the authority and sufficiency of the Bible for understanding doctrine:

> The Protestant emphasis on *sola scriptura*, the letter of Scripture as the basis of true doctrine, suggested that accumulations of Catholic visions and revelation concerning angels must be disregarded. . . . Calvin raises the subject of angels and immediately proceeds to what *should not* be believed.[46]

Calvin's most extensive presentation on angelology is in Book 1, chapter 14 of the *Institutes of the Christian Religion* (1559 ed.). Among the topics Calvin considers are:

- The superiority of Scripture over speculation regarding angels (1.14.4)
- The designation of angels in Scripture (1.14.5)
- The angels as protectors and helpers of believers (1.14.6)
- The question of guardian angels (1.14.7)
- The hierarchy, number, and forms of the angels (1.14.8)
- The reality of angels (1.14.9)
- The absence of the divine glory for angels (1.14.10)
- The use of the angels by God (1.14.11)
- The potential of diverting the believer's attention from Christ to angels (1.14.12)
- The reality of Satan and demons as adversaries (1.14.13–19; see also 2.4.1–5)

Calvin rejects the idea that the hierarchies of angels can be known in the manner that the work of Pseudo-Dionysius had portrayed.

He rejects praying to angels and asking for angelic assistance. To him, speculation about angels diverted the Christian from God and made the Christian susceptible to satanic deception. Too much speculation leads to vanity and, as a result, people become misled in their worship of God. Calvin believed that much of the information about angels was part of the "secret things" that "belong to the LORD our God" (Deut. 29:29). Because of this idea, he declared: "If we would be duly wise, we must leave those empty speculations which idle men have taught apart from God's Word concerning the nature, orders, and numbers of angels."[47]

Raymond writes of Calvin's view: "God is comprehended through the Incarnation, and understanding angels does not for Calvin, as it did for Augustine, Aquinas, and even Luther, bring us any closer to knowing God. Angels perform God's offices, but do so more as efficient secretaries than as mysterious and benign witnesses of human drama."[48] Similarly, Soergel writes:

> Calvin's statements about the angels dismissed the long and distinguished legacy of medieval angelology that had flourished among scholastic theologians from the thirteenth to the sixteenth centuries. . . . In the high and later Middle Ages angelology had matured as a discipline because it could become a complete vehicle for explaining the precise mechanism by which God acted on earth and in the cosmos. Angels being divided into their distinctive ranks, charged with controlling different functions in the universe and with ministering to earthly dominions and individuals, angelology flourished as a way of answering precise questions about how God dealt with humankind in his creation.[49]

Angels were very real and were messengers from God, but excessive contemplation of them was thought to be counterproductive to spiritual maturation and the true worship of God.

The Reformers strongly believed angels were an integral part of the world providentially created and sustained by God. This was a world in which, as the Bible taught, not a single sparrow perished or hair fell without divine knowledge, permission, and active intervention. Yet just why an omnipotent God should choose to act by proxy through angels in declaring or affecting His will was something that must remain unknown to the redeemed in this lifetime. The Reformers acknowledged that angels were sometimes used as messengers and also at times as heralds and instruments of vengeance and punishment.[50] However, the Reformers believed that God usually used these divine messengers for things that humans would consider more constructive than destructive. The busy ministry of the angels to humans was a sign of God's love for the faithful in this world. The angels performed their ministries because God, understanding human needs and frailties, directed them out of His love and grace to do so.[51] The presence of the angels is a perpetual reminder of God's love and grace.

41. What is the meaning of the phrase "angels dancing on the head of a pin"?

The question of how many angels can dance or sit on the head of a pin is used sometimes to demean and dismiss the angelology and theology of medieval Scholasticism as represented in the thought of theologians such as Thomas Aquinas (1225–1274) and Duns Scotus (ca. 1265–1308). The origins of the statement are unclear. In daily conversations the question is used derogatorily when a discussion or presentation is considered pedantic or obscure. Some people think that it was first articulated by Protestant Reformers such as Martin Luther (1483–1546) and John Calvin (1509–1564) in disparaging comments about the methods and theology of the earlier theologians.[52] Others believe it may have been fabricated in the seventeenth century by a group of philosophers known as the Cambridge Platonists and argue that it was never uttered by the Scholastics.[53] And they are probably correct with regard to the Scholastics. There was, however, an anonymous but well-known fourteenth-century mystical writing known as *Schwester Katrei* (*Sister Catherine*) that refers to a "thousand souls sitting in heaven on a needlepoint."[54]

One of the earliest known usages of the phrase is from English churchman William Chillingsworth (1602–1644) who, in his 1638 book *The Religion of Protestants a Safe Way to Salvation*, writes of Protestants that "they dispute not eternally 'Whether a Million of Angels may not fit upon a needles point?' Because they fill not their brains with notions that signify nothing."[55] Another early usage is by a famous Puritan minister. In his 1667 book *The Reasons of the Christian Religion*, English Puritan divine Richard Baxter (1615–1691) reviewed opinions on the corporeal and material nature of angels from the medieval era, concluding "And Schibler [?] with others, maketh the difference of extension to be this, that Angels *can contract their whole substance into one part of space, and therefore have not partes extra partes.* Whereupon it is that the Schoolmen have questioned how many Angels may fit upon the point of a Needle?"[56] Whether a parody or an actual question, the issue of angels on the head of a pin is not as ludicrous as it might seem.

After the rediscovery in the twelfth century of the works of Greek philosophers such as Aristotle and Plato, medieval theologians sought to reconcile Greek philosophical concepts with Christian theology. This resulted in the Scholastic method wherein Christian orthodoxy was studied and defended through dialectical reasoning, the use of inference, and the attempted resolution of contradictions. This was often done in a question and answer format whose primary purpose was to find an answer to a question or resolve a philosophical and theological contradiction. The Scholastics viewed themselves as theologians rather than philosophers.

Issues discussed during the era by the Scholastics focused on the nature of God, the purpose of theology and metaphysics, and philosophical issues concerning the problem of knowledge, of universals, and of individuation or identity. It was, in part, because of the content and method of these highly technical discussions and inquiries that Thomas Aquinas, following the thought of an earlier theologian, Peter Damian (1007–1072), argued that philosophy is the "handmaiden of theology" and thus subservient to it as an academic discipline. Among earlier Scholastics were Peter Abelard (1079–1142), Anselm of Canterbury (1033–1109), and Lanfranc of Canterbury (ca. 1005–1089).

In later centuries, the medieval era in general and Scholasticism in particular were treated disparagingly by the Renaissance humanists, who saw this as a barbaric "middle" period (thus, the term "Middle Ages") between the classical age of Greek and Roman culture and the "rebirth" or *renaissance* of classical culture and a devaluing of theology.

Although Aquinas did not ever use the phrase about angels and a pin, he did question in his *Summa theologica* whether it was possible or likely for more than one angel to occupy the same space. His answer is no. "There are not two angels in the same place. . . . There can be but one angel in one place" (Part 1, Q. 52, art. 3).

If one takes theology and the Bible seriously, then it is not unreasonable to ask about the relationship between the spiritual world and the material world—body and soul, matter and spirit. And in so doing, several questions arise with regard to angels and several options or lines of thought are open to those who inquire. That is exactly what the Scholastics were trying to do in their inquiries, even if they didn't ask about angels and pins. Do angels occupy space? If so, what is the most or least amount of space required for one angel? Can angels be in more than one place at a time? Questions such as these prompt Christians to consider the relationship between science and theology as well as philosophy and theology. These are not matters to be taken lightly or ridiculed!

42. Why are angels portrayed in art with wings, harps, and halos?

In both Byzantine and Latin Christianity, there is a rich history of religious art. This has given rise over the centuries to many vibrant and different representations of biblical figures and history, and especially of Jesus Christ. Religious art often reflected theological controversies and doctrines of the period, and for almost every area of doctrine, there is corresponding art. In angelology, it is often vivid and moving.

According to Isaiah 6:1–5, the seraphim have wings as do the cherubim seen by Ezekiel in his vision (1:6). Exodus 25:20 also describes representations of them with wings over the ark of the covenant. Moreover, the angels John saw as recorded in Revelation 4:8 had wings. This does not mean, however, that all angels have wings, even in their invisible spirit nature; on that the Bible is silent, and most of the appearances of angels in the Bible are in human form.

The earliest portrayals in Christian art from the third century depict angels as young men without wings, but by the fourth century Christian art begins to show them with wings. Perhaps there was some artistic influence from depictions of pagan images such as Mercury, Eros, and Nike. However, the biblical imagery of angels as swift-moving beings was well-established in Judaism and Christianity and likely also influenced representations of them (cf. 2 Sam. 22:11; Pss. 18:10; 104:3) and by the time of Tertullian (ca. 160–220), angels as winged beings was widely accepted.[57]

The iconography of the halo is associated with many traditions, including Greek and Roman mythology and history. In Christian art it begins to appear by the fourth century, especially in representations of Christ, emphasizing the divine nature of Christ. The halo is a symbol of holiness and the glory of God and the light and radiance often associated with it in biblical texts. The idea of halos on angels dates from the fifth century.

Nowhere in the Bible are angels depicted as playing harps (though in Rev. 8:2 a trumpet is blown). But the harp is a biblical instrument and mentioned several times in Psalms (33:2; 57:8; 71:22; 81:2–3; 92:3). In Psalm 148, the angels are urged to praise God with music, though without mention of harps. The portrayal of angels with harps probably comes from their association (or confusion) with the saints in heaven, who are depicted with harps in Revelation 15:2 (cf. 14:2). Angels playing harps and other musical instruments became popular in art from the twelfth century onward.[58]

43. Is there an angel of death?

There are certainly images of angels destroying the enemies of God and being present at moments of death (cf. Exod. 12:23; 2 Sam. 24:16; 2 Kings 19:35). Also, in the seal judgments of Revelation 6:1–8, the fourth horseman is ashen or pale in color and brings death to much of the world's population (6:7–8). However, we do not find biblical support for a sentient spiritual being who causes death, leads victims to death, or is present at the moment of death as its sole function. Portrayal of angels, fallen and unfallen, at the moment of death is a theme that has been part of Christian angelology and art for centuries.[59] We believe that angels are present at the death of the redeemed (Luke 16:22), but there is no specific fallen angel that is a death angel.

In the instance of Exodus 12:23, the "destroyer" may have been the Angel of the Lord, the pre-incarnate Christ: "For the LORD will pass through to smite the Egyptians; and when He sees the blood on the lintel and on the two doorposts, the LORD will pass over the door and will not allow the destroyer to come in to your houses to smite you" (see also 1 Chron. 21:15).

Two passages sometimes considered in support of an angel of death are Job 33:22 and Proverbs 16:14. The passage in Job, "Then his soul draws near to the pit, and his life to those who bring death," is likely a reference to a belief in demons thought to cause death and not angels. Nor do we see an angel of death in Proverbs 16:14: "The fury of a king is like messengers of death, but a wise man will appease it." Rather, the verse is simply stating the idea that a king's wrath threatens death.

Throughout the history of Christianity, there have been strong images in art and literature of the personification of death and angels of death. Sometimes the archangel Michael is portrayed as a good angel of death as opposed to Samael (a figure from Talmudic and post-Talmudic lore, who is understood either as a fallen angel of death or an unfallen angel with duties pertaining to death). However, these portrayals are not biblically based. The angel of death appears many times in Renaissance art in works such as those of Albrecht Dürer (1471–1528).

There was in Greek mythology the idea of death being personified in the daemon known as Thanatos (a daemon being a good or benevolent supernatural being). It was the job of Thanatos to escort the departed to the underworld where he would hand them over to Charon who ferried the departed across the river Acheron that separated the living from the dead. Charon is likely the precursor of the images of the Grim Reaper that became popular in folklore from the fifteenth century onward.

In Judaism there is a history of belief in an angel of death, and there are numerous references in the Midrash, Talmud, and subsequent rabbinic literature.[60] Islam also has a strong tradition in an angel of death. Despite these traditions, there is no biblical support for an angel of death.

44. How did the writings of John Milton and other English writers influence views about angels?

John Milton's *Paradise Lost* is certainly one of the most important and famous pieces of English literature ever written. The story of *Paradise Lost* is told by angels and involves their communications, actions, and conflict throughout the work—it is, in short, a poem about angels. It was also a very influential poem in seventeenth-century Protestant Britain. "The force of his poem lies in a narrative taut enough to knit together story and doctrine and a language capacious enough to speak angelology and poetry at the same time."[61] But Milton (1608–1674) was not the only literary figure in England to write of angels. Literary predecessors John

Donne (1572–1631) and Edmund Spenser (1552–1559) also wrote extensively of angels, and the writings of all three men are infused with biblical imagery and Protestant theology.[62] However, they were not constrained by theology when creating their masterpieces and, therefore, orthodoxy is not always found in the details of their writings. For example, Milton's angels consume food and are capable of sexual relations with one another.[63]

Summarizing Milton's writings of angels in *Paradise Lost*, Diane McColley writes:

> Raphael recounts the war in heaven and the creation of the world to Adam and Eve in rich images accommodated to their understanding and gives Adam counsel on knowledge, nurture, and divine, human, and angelic love. Michael shows in vision and narrative the consequences of the Fall and the prophetic history of redemption. Abdiel furnishes the angelic model of heroic choice, and Gabriel, Uriel, Zephon, Ithuriel, and Zophiel take an active part. Among the fallen angels, Satan, Beelzebub, Moloch, Mammon, and Beliel oppose hate, vandalism and degeneracy to the joyful service and resplendent arts of dance and hymnody in which the unfallen fellowship delights.[64]

Milton uses biblical stories as a foundation for his works, but he does not hesitate to go beyond the stories and biblical teaching in the creation of his literary pieces. His influence and the influence of others is not so much in the details of his angelology as in the acceptance of angels as a reality. Through writings such as *Paradise Lost*, angels became part of British Protestant culture outside boundaries of theological discussion and spirituality. English writers brought to an English-speaking audience an appreciation and acceptance of angels as a reality and as beings worthy of the literary imagination.

PART 3

Angels, Satan, and Demons in the World Today

45. How do angels relate to Christians?

The New Testament records a wide and diverse angelic ministry to the redeemed, and there is no reason to think that such ministry does not exist today. The author of Hebrews, after declaring the superiority of Christ over the angels and demonstrating it from Old Testament passages in Deuteronomy and Psalms, rhetorically asks his readers in Hebrews 1:14: "Are they not all ministering spirits, sent out to render service for the sake of those who will inherit salvation?" In this brief statement we have one of the clearest biblical statements on the nature and purpose of angels today—spirits sent from God to minister through service to the redeemed of God on earth who are awaiting the culmination of their redemption (cf. 1 John 3:2). Angels carry out tasks as agents of God, ministering spirits, and divine emissaries.

At times, God chooses to use angels to accomplish His purposes according to His will. Because He is omnipotent, angelic service is not mandatory for the accomplishing of God's will but, rather, a method that at times God chooses to use. God can accomplish His will apart from angels and intervene directly in the lives of believers, however, He often chooses to use angels. Even so, it is important to remember that angels are not the source of the ministry and, therefore, are not to be worshipped (Col. 2:18).

Ministry During the Life of the Believer

There are many instances in the Bible of angels serving as watchers or witnesses of earthly events, both great and small. For the Christian today that can be a source of great comfort and consolation. Angels see our victories and our defeats, spiritually and physically. Paul wrote that angels witnessed the suffering of the apostles (1 Cor. 4:9). He also wrote that the angels observed the worship of Christians and the plan of God for the church (1 Cor. 11:10; Eph. 3:10). Similarly, Peter wrote that angels eagerly desire ("long to look") to see the work of Christ, God's plan unfolding in history through the preaching of the gospel, and the fulfillment of prophecy (1 Peter 1:12).

Luke's gospel records Jesus' teaching that just as a shepherd rejoices over finding a lost sheep or a woman rejoices when she finds a lost coin, so do the angels rejoice when an individual repents (Luke 15:7, 10). Angels see and know of the conversion of every person.

After a person's salvation, angels are at times used by God as encouragers, especially in times of danger. Such an instance is recorded in Acts 27 where we read of an angel encouraging Paul during his difficult voyage and shipwreck as he journeyed to Rome as a prisoner. At one point in the voyage, after seeing an angel, Paul spoke to the crew and passengers foretelling the grounding and destruction of the ship. Luke records Paul's words:

> Yet now I urge you to keep up your courage, for there will be no loss of life among you, but only of the ship. For this very night an angel of the God to whom I belong and whom I serve stood before me, saying, "Do not be afraid, Paul; you

must stand before Caesar; and behold, God has granted you all those who are sailing with you." Therefore, keep up your courage, men, for I believe God that it will turn out exactly as I have been told. But we must run aground on a certain island. (Acts 27:22–26)

The island was Malta (Acts 28:1) and everything came to pass just as the angel and Paul said it would. In this instance, the ministry of the angel was directly to Paul and indirectly to all who were aboard the ship. Was this a special angel sent to Paul or the work of a guardian angel? We don't know, however, this example of angelic ministry fits just as well with perceptions and belief regarding the ministry of guardian angels as it does with the idea that angels are sent at certain times to minister to individuals (cf. Ps. 91:11–12).

One of the primary activities of angels is to praise and worship God (Ps. 148:1–2; Isa. 6:3; Heb. 1:6; Rev. 5:8–13; 7:9–12). In so doing, they serve as a model and continual reminder to Christians of the glory, majesty, and power of God. When some of the angels rebelled against God, there was no redemption for them (2 Peter 2:4; Jude 6), but God has chosen to redeem human beings who also have sinned and turned against Him (Heb. 2:16; Rev. 5:9). Thus the angels, unfallen and fallen, are a perpetual reminder of God's love and of the salvation that is available to us (John 3:16). When we serve God we do so in the presence of angels and with them as witnesses, just as Paul reminded Timothy, saying, "I solemnly charge you in the presence of God and of Christ Jesus and of His chosen angels, to maintain these principles without bias, doing nothing in a spirit of partiality" (1 Tim. 5:21).

Is it possible to be unaware of angelic presence and ministry? Yes, it is possible. That is exactly what happened when Balaam encountered an angel. According to an amazing account in Numbers 22:22–36, Balaam's donkey recognized the angel even though Balaam did not see it. In another instance in the Old Testament, the prophet Elisha was able to see a vast angelic army while his attendant could not see the angels (2 Kings 6:15–17). In Hebrews 13 readers are encouraged to be mindful of social responsibilities, especially with respect to strangers. The author alludes to the story of Abraham unknowingly entertaining angels that he thought were strangers (Gen. 18), writing, "Do not neglect to show hospitality to strangers, for by this some have entertained angels without knowing it" (Heb. 13:2).

Whether they appear in the form of humans and come in dreams as they did to Jacob (Gen. 31:10–13) and Joseph (Matt. 1:20–25; 2:13–15, 19–23), Christians should be mindful of the possibility of angelic presence. The result of such awareness and sensitivity to the realm of spiritual beings is obedience to the instructions of God. At the same time, Christians must also be mindful of the possibility of deception by Satan (2 Cor. 11:14; Gal. 1:8).

Ministry at the Death of the Believer

We have probably all sung or heard the stanza in "Swing Low, Sweet Chariot," the well-known American spiritual:

> I looked over Jordan, and what did I see,
>   Coming for to carry me home?
> A band of angels coming after me,
>   Coming for to carry me home.

The often-sung song tells of freedom from adversity. Wallace Willis, a Native-American freedman from the Choctaw tribe living in what was then Indian Territory and is now Oklahoma, wrote the lyrics around 1862. He was inspired by viewing the Red River, which reminded him of the Jordan River and of the biblical story of the prophet Elijah being taken to heaven by a chariot (2 Kings 2:11). The imagery of the words is the unmistakable journey of angels carrying a person to heaven.

Though much of the imagery of the song is found in the Old Testament, there is the very powerful parable told by Jesus and recorded in Luke 16 of angels carrying to "Abraham's bosom" (the presence of God) a beggar named Lazarus when he died (Luke 16:19–22). The parable of Lazarus and the rich man is a powerful story of wealth, death, judgment, and the afterlife. Interestingly, Lazarus is the only person named in any of the parables and stories of Jesus. The concept of angelic escort to heaven at the time of death was a common image in Jewish literature (as was the possibility of satanic escort to hell).[1] Jesus does not question or deny the belief of angelic ministry at death. Do such things really happen? We believe that angels are present at the death of the believer and part of the process of instantaneous transformation of the believer into the presence of God (2 Cor. 5:8). Though not visible to all who may be present, their ministry is occurring.

46. How do angels relate to non-Christians?

Most of what the Bible teaches about angels concerns their interactions and ministry to Old Testament saints or New Testament believers. Though angels appeared to the shepherds announcing the birth of Jesus, there is no reason to think that the shepherds were unbelievers in the Old Testament sense—certainly their response shows them to be men of faith awaiting the arrival of the Savior and Messiah (Luke 2:15, 20). There is little in the Bible to support an idea of continual angelic interaction with non-Christians. This does not mean that such things do not happen but, rather, that there is minimal biblical teaching on the subject and therefore we must be cautious in our conjectures. There is more evidence of the work of fallen angels (demons) in the lives of nonbelievers than there is of angels who did not fall with Satan.

We must not confuse the work of angels with the work of the Holy Spirit in the lives of non-Christians (or Christians). It is the Holy Spirit who convicts individuals of sin (John 16:8–11), regenerates (Titus 3:5), indwells (1 Cor. 6:19), and baptizes (1 Cor. 12:13). In Acts 8:26–39 there is the account of an angel participating in the evangelizing of an Ethiopian by the apostle Philip, but it is to Philip that the angel appears and speaks rather than to the Ethiopian.

However, we do know from the Bible that angels are part of the process of judgment on the unrighteous, both in the past (Gen. 19:13; Acts 12:23) and in the future (Matt. 13:39–40; Rev. 14:6–7; 16:1; 19:17–18). These verses stand as a reminder and warning that angels are not the benign and sentimental creatures so often portrayed in our culture but are messengers of God responding to His words and will.

47. How do demons relate to Christians?

Demons can and do attack and harass Christians, but because Christians are "in Christ" (e.g., Rom. 6:23; 8:1–2; 16:3, 7; 1 Cor. 1:2, 30; Gal. 3:28) and have the indwelling presence of the Holy Spirit (John 7:39; Acts 11:16–17; Rom. 5:5; 1 Cor. 2:12; 6:19; 2 Cor. 5:5), we do not believe that Christians can be demon-possessed. In 1 Corinthians 6:19, Paul writes, "Or do you not know that your body is a temple of the Holy Spirit who is in you, whom you have from God, and that you are not your own?" If the Holy Spirit lives in the Christian, how then can a demon enter the believer's physical body and take control of it? There are no incidents of demon possession of Christians recorded in the Bible. However, Christians can be externally influenced by demons and oppressed by them.[2] John writes in 1 John 4:4 "greater is He [the Holy Spirit] who is in you than he who is in the world [Satan]" (cf. John 12:31). Similarly, in 2 Thessalonians 3:3 Paul writes: "But the Lord is faithful, and He will strengthen and protect you from the evil one." The protection of the believer is based on the faithfulness of God, not the faithfulness of the individual Christian. While not all evangelical scholars who have written extensively on angels and demons agree with our view (cf. Dickason and Unger), we believe that it is consistent with the teaching of the Bible.

Personal sin in the lives of Christians is not due to external activity by demons but to the sin nature that is in every person. Paul frequently uses the term "the flesh" to indicate this condition (cf. Rom. 7:14, 18; 8:1–17; Gal. 3:3; 5:13–21; Eph. 2:3). We cannot shift the blame to someone or something else either physical or spiritual.

What then can demons do to Christians? In addition to the many ways Satan attacks believers,[3] the fallen angels who follow him are also active in opposing the redeemed and in spreading spiritual deceit:

- Demons may hinder answers to prayers. Though we do not have a New Testament example of this, in Daniel 10:12–20 Daniel is told by an angel (likely Gabriel) that a supernatural being known as the "prince of the kingdom of Persia" tried to oppose God's plan and Daniel's prayer. This came about as a result of angelic warfare between the archangel Michael, the guardian of Israel (12:1), and a fallen angel opposing him for a period of three weeks (10:13).[4]

- Demons, in conjunction with Satan, attempt to thwart Christians. In Matthew 25:41, Jesus says that eternal punishment awaits "the devil and his angels"—that is, those who aligned themselves with Satan and his spiritual warfare against God in heaven and on earth. In Ephesians 6:12, Paul reminds Christians that they are involved in spiritual warfare against Satan's angels, "the spiritual forces of wickedness in the heavenly places." Of this spiritual warfare, New Testament scholar Harold Hoehner noted: "Although Christ has won the victory at the cross, the reality of conflict presently continues for the believers. The fact that Paul instructs believers to put on the armor of God argues for the present reality of the struggle. . . . Positionally believers have victory in Christ in the heavenlies, but in reality the victory will not be fully realized until the subjugation of evil yet in the future."[5]

- Demons, in futility, wish to separate the Christian from Jesus Christ and the eternal security that Christians have because of the love and work of Christ (Rom. 8:28–29).

- Demons attempt to create jealousy in and divisions among Christians. Demons cannot steal Christians away from Christ, but they can neutralize their spiritual growth and unity (James 3:13–16).

Robert Dean and Thomas Ice summarize well the nature of spiritual warfare in relation to Satan and his demons:

> True spiritual warfare is focused primarily on the world and the flesh, not on preoccupation with demons. The focus of the Christian should be on proper ethical conduct in accordance with God's Word, not on a metaphysical battle with Satan and his demons. . . . The call for today is to let the Bible tell us who our real enemy is, what our battle plan involves, and how to carry it out. As Christians, we must be completely submissive to Jesus Christ and His Word. Satan wants you to get your eyes on him; God wants you to get your eyes on Him and His Word.[6]

In his letter to Christians at Colossae (in present-day Turkey), Paul wrote of God's spiritual protection of believers: "For He rescued us from the domain of darkness, and transferred us to the kingdom of His beloved Son" (Col. 1:13). Demons and their attacks on Christians are very real, but not all physical, psychological, emotional, or spiritual problems are demon-related. Most are likely not demon-related, however, such attacks do occur and, therefore, Christians must be alert and discerning. The works of Satan and his demons can be successfully resisted and defeated by Christians (James 4:7; 1 John 4:4).

48. How do demons relate to non-Christians?

The goal of demonic activity is to hinder the purpose of God for humanity and to extend the power and work of Satan. They work to mislead and destroy the unsaved through spiritual and physical means. In so doing, they willingly cooperate with Satan in his ongoing rebellion against God and through his counterfeit spiritual activities on earth. There are numerous accounts of demonic activity in the four gospels during the ministry of Jesus and in the history of the early church as recorded in the book of Acts. From these incidents as well as from the teaching found in the Old Testament, attacks and affliction by demons can take many forms. Like Satan, they are created beings with extensive but limited powers. They are not omniscient, omnipresent, or omnipotent, even though at times the breadth and scope of their work seems to indicate otherwise (cf. Isa. 46:9–10; Mark 13:32). They affect non-Christians through deception and affliction. According to the Bible, among their actions:

- Demons participate in the activities and plans of Satan, known as the "deep things of Satan" in his opposition to God (Rev. 2:24; contrast those things with "the depths of God" in 1 Cor. 2:10).
- Demons follow and mimic the actions of Satan (John 8:44).
- Demons deceive people promoting false doctrine (1 Cor. 12:3; 1 Tim. 4:1).
- Demons influence false prophets (1 John 4:1–4).
- Demons promote false religion (1 John 4:1–4).
- Demons deny the validity of the incarnation, work, and ascension of Jesus Christ (1 Tim. 3:16–4:1).
- Demons promote idolatry (Lev. 17:7; Deut. 32:17; Ps. 106:36–38; 1 Cor. 10:20; Rev. 9:20).
- Demons at times are involved the affairs of nations (Dan. 10:13; Rev. 13:13–16).
- Demons may inflict individuals physically (Matt. 9:33; 12:22; 17:14–18; Luke 13:11).
- Demons may inflict individuals psychologically and cause self-destructive behavior (Mark 5:4–5; 9:22; Luke 8:27–29; 9:37–42).
- Demons may be involved in the death of individuals (Rev. 9:14–19).
- Demons may possess individuals, controlling their actions and

thoughts for destructive purposes, at times giving them excessive strength and abilities (Mark 1:23–26; 5:1–4; 9:17–18, 20, 22).

- Demons may enter and destroy animals (Mark 5:13).
- Demons working with Satan may produce false miracles (2 Thess. 2:9).

Not all evil and sin in the world is due to Satan or demons, but some of it is and there needs to be an awareness of the reality and nature of the spiritual warfare that occurs in the world. Satan and his demons will not be victorious, but the battles are, and will be, long and hard.

49. Does every person have a guardian angel?

Although it is not uniformly held, belief in guardian angels is a long-standing idea in Christianity dating to the earliest years of the faith (and in Judaism before that).[7] The view that individuals had personal spirits or deities to guide them was also part of other religious and philosophical systems in the ancient world. Apart from noncanonical writings in early Christianity, five primary biblical passages are used to support the view:

> He blessed Joseph, and said, "The God before whom my fathers Abraham and Isaac walked, the God who has been my shepherd all my life to this day, the angel who has redeemed me from all evil, bless the lads; And may my name live on in them, and the names of my fathers Abraham and Isaac; and may they grow into a multitude in the midst of the earth." (Gen. 48:15–16)

> For He will give His angels charge concerning you,
> To guard you in all your ways.
> They will bear you up in their hands,
> that you do not strike your foot against a stone.
> (Ps. 91:11–12)

See that you do not despise one of these little ones, for I say to you that their angels in heaven continually see the face of My Father who is in heaven. (Matt. 18:10)

They said to her, "You are out of your mind!" But she kept insisting that it was so. They kept saying, "It is his angel." (Acts 12:15; at least for the redeemed)

Are they not all ministering spirits, sent out to render service for the sake of those who will inherit salvation? (Heb. 1:14)

Of these five, the words of Jesus in Matthew 18:10 are the ones most commonly used in support of guardian angels. In Roman Catholicism and Eastern Orthodoxy, there is additionally an appeal to the book of *Tobit*, a writing not considered canonical by Protestants:

And the holy Angel of the Lord, Raphael, was sent to care for both of them, whose prayers were recited at the same time in the sight of the Lord. (*Tobit* 3:25)

In Matthew's passage Jesus appears to be gesturing toward a child who was nearby (cf. 18:2). It may indeed be that Jesus is stating that each child has a guardian angel, but Jesus may also be saying simply that angels assigned the mission of protecting children, not necessarily individual guardian angels, have access to God the Father. Similarly, the reference to an angel guarding Peter in Acts 12:15 may not be a personal guardian angel assigned to Peter throughout his life but rather an angel assigned the task of protecting him during that specific time.

There is a long and rich tradition of Christian belief in guardian angels, but there is nothing in the Bible that definitively proves or disproves their existence as angels whose sole function is the protection of a specific individual. Belief or disbelief regarding them is not a central doctrine of faith and is an area where there is room for agreement, disagreement, or uncertainty. On this subject we side with John Calvin, who wrote: "But whether individual angels have been assigned to individual believers for their protection, I dare not affirm with confidence."[8]

50. Do those who die become angels?

Angels are not deceased humans with wings and halos, nor are demons deceased humans with a pitchfork and horns. When a person dies, Christian or otherwise, they do not become an angel (nor do angels ever become human, even though at times they may appear as humans). Even though popular culture, movies, art, and songs sometimes portray the deceased as angels, this is contrary to what the Bible says about them (Matt. 22:30; Mark 12:25). Angels are not glorified humans (cf. Heb. 12:22–23 where angels and spirits of the righteous are differentiated).[9] Angels and humans share some qualities and have some similarities such as intellect and will, but they also have distinct and perpetual differences; for example, humans are created in the image of God and angels are not. In heaven, Christians will have a recognizable spiritual and resurrection body just like Jesus Christ possessed after the resurrection (1 Cor. 15:50–53; Phil. 3:21; 1 John 3:2).

We believe that even those who have experienced the death of a child, albeit through circumstances such as miscarriage or abortion, will know them as they might have been had they lived longer. How this occurs and at what age the child will appear is unclear from the Bible, but we know that God is just and loving and acts accordingly and will not punish those who were never able to receive and reject the offer of salvation. These individuals, regardless of their age at death, are human beings and not angels.[10]

Just as people do not become angels, neither does the Bible teach that they become ghosts. What most people consider to be a ghost, a disembodied spirit of a human, is probably a demonic manifestation and what the Bible normally calls an evil spirit. The account of a witch calling up the spirit of Samuel (1 Sam. 28:7–20) is an unusual story wherein God permitted Samuel to speak to Saul at the instigation of a medium who normally drew on the demonic powers of necromancy (Duet. 18:10–11). The fact that the woman was surprised when an apparition of Samuel appeared indicated that she was not expecting a true encounter with Samuel (28:12–14). Those who engage in such practices, like the medium of Endor, have no true power over the deceased. They can only produce counterfeit experiences through the aid of demons.

Humans were created to be embodied beings while angels were created to be incorporeal spirit beings; they are never said to be created in the image of God as are humans. Those who die in Christ are immediately and consciously in the presence of God without the resurrection bodies that they will receive at the rapture (Luke 23:43; 1 Cor. 15:12–57; 2 Cor. 5:6–8).

51. What is the difference between the work of angels and the work of the Holy Spirit?

Angels and the Holy Spirit both minister to individuals, but the nature of those ministries is very different. Angels are ministering spirits sent from God as divine messengers (Heb. 1:14). The Holy Spirit is God, the third person of the Trinity (Matt. 28:19; Acts 5:3–4; 2 Cor. 13:14). The chasm between God and the angels is enormous, and the Creator/creature distinctions can never be bridged. The ministry of angels is primarily external to the individual, whereas the work of the Holy Spirit is primarily internal to the individual. In addition to the indwelling, baptizing, and filling works of the Holy Spirit (1 Cor. 6:19; 12:13; Eph. 5:18), the Holy Spirit performs numerous other works and ministries. Among those ministries are teaching (John 16:12–15), guiding (Rom. 8:14), assuring (Rom. 8:16), and praying (Rom. 8:26). The Holy Spirit and the angels are both very present in the world and the lives of people, but in very different ways and for very different reasons.

52. How will the redeemed relate to angels in heaven?

The redeemed will participate in the future judgment of fallen angels and will also join with the unfallen angels in eternal praise of God. Paul tells the Christians at Corinth that they will one day judge the angels: "Or do you not know that the saints will judge the world? If the world is judged by you, are you not competent to constitute the smallest law courts? Do you not know that we will judge angels? How much more matters of this life?" (1 Cor. 6:2–3). Because of their union with Christ, they will be associated with the judgments Christ carries out at the end of the millennium (cf. Matt. 19:28). Part of this judgment process entails the final judgment of Satan and the fallen angels (Matt. 25:41; 2 Peter 2:4; Jude 6; Rev. 20:10), and it is those angels Paul is referencing in the 1 Corinthians verses.

In heaven, with resurrection bodies, we will recognize and understand spiritual matters precisely as they exist. Our comprehension will be total, though not infinite, and unhindered by a sinful nature. We will see the angels and fully understand them (1 Cor. 13:12). We will also worship with them. This is described in great detail in Revelation 7:9–12:

> After these things I looked, and behold, a great multitude which no one could count, from every nation and all tribes and peoples and tongues, standing before the throne and before the Lamb, clothed in white robes, and palm branches *were* in their hands; and they cry out with a loud voice, saying, "Salvation to our God who sits on the throne, and to the Lamb."
>
> And all the angels were standing around the throne and *around* the elders and the four living creatures; and they fell on their faces before the throne and worshiped God, saying, "Amen, blessing and glory and wisdom and thanksgiving and honor and power and might, be to our God forever and ever. Amen."

The most glorious of all angelic encounters will be one that is everlasting as we join with all of the angels in the eternal praise of God. The magnificence of this praise and worship is incomprehensible to us today, but it will come to pass, for as Paul reminded the Corinthians, "just as it is written, 'things which eye has not seen and ear has not heard, and which have not entered the heart of man, all that God has prepared for those who love Him'" (1 Cor. 2:9).

53. Why should we care about angels and demons?

Scripture teaches the existence and work of angels and demons, and all Scripture is given for our benefit (2 Tim. 3:15–17). We need to be ready to give an answer for our faith and our beliefs. In so doing, we proclaim the message and truths of Christianity to an often confused, needy, and deceived world. In the pages of Scripture, we find an authoritative and balanced presentation of the spirit world—the world of angels and demons. In his extensive study of biblical angelology, C. Fred Dickason presents six helpful reminders as to why we should care about angels and demons. If we understand the biblical perspective of the spirit world:

1. We increase our appreciation of a sovereign God who creatively controls the universe and intervenes on our behalf for His glory and good.
2. We gain comfort through the ministry of angels that God uses to further demonstrate (beyond the death of Christ on the cross for us) His intensely personal love for us.
3. We further understand and appreciate the holiness and righteousness of God, knowing that all beings in heaven and earth are subject to certain judgment.
4. We gain insight into the grace of God who chooses not to judge all sin at once, but is patient.
5. We gain greater awareness of the realities of the spiritual life and the forces at play in the life of every person.

6. We gain encouragement about and assurance of the love and protection of God for every believer.[11]

Understanding what the Bible teaches about angels gives us a reality check for facing temptation and trials in this world. It is a reminder that there is ongoing spiritual warfare in the world in which we and the angels (fallen and unfallen) partake. Additionally, it is important for us to understand the ministry of angels because their worship of God is an example for us in our worship of God. Angels are present in the world as messengers, guides, exemplars, and protectors. We also serve as examples to the angels who are always watching the events on earth. "God's desire for you is that you should obey His will, that you should believe His Word, and that you should worship His Person just as Jesus Christ did. You can be an object lesson for God to the angels through your submission, through your faith, through your worship that He is God and beside Him there is no other."[12]

PART 4

Angels, Satan, and Demons in World Religions

54. What do Judaism and the mystical tradition of Kabbalah teach about angels?

Judaism has a rich and broad history of angelology spanning many centuries and, as in the history of Christianity, there is no monolithic perspective through the centuries. Yet, as in Christianity, angels are created beings who serve as messengers of God, worship God, and function as ministering spirits. Angels are not worshipped and are not the focus of devotion. In addition to the teaching regarding angels found in the Hebrew Scriptures (Christian Old Testament), there is a rich and extensive history and literature of angelology in Judaism.[1] Sources for information about angels and demons include the Apocrypha and Pseudepigrapha, the Dead Sea Scrolls, the Talmud, the *Zohar*, and medieval literature such as the Sefer Hasidim. The tradition and theology of angelology developed more fully during the Second Temple era (515 B.C.–A.D. 70). During the time of Jesus, the Sadducees denied the existence of angels, but the Pharisees upheld the belief (Acts 23:8).[2]

The Essenes at Qumran had a highly defined angelology, and

angels are often found in apocryphal literature that is not part of the either Hebrew Scripture or the Bible as Christians understand it, such as the books of the Maccabees or the apocalyptic *Book of Enoch*. In *Enoch* 3 there is a long list of angels with various functions, naming angels as those in charge of thunder, earthquakes, hail, snow, and the sea. There is, however, no uniform view of the nature and character of angels in these writings.[3] These apocalyptic writings are filled with angelic activity and the end of days. In the Dead Sea Scrolls found at Qumran, there is also extensive mention of angels, especially in the "Manual of Discipline" that speaks of an angel of light and an angel of darkness. Although these views are not part of the Jewish Bible, some of the ideas were incorporated in rabbinic literature and became part of later Jewish mysticism.[4]

In Jewish nonbiblical apocalyptic thought, there was a hierarchy and groupings of angels such as Michael, Gabriel, and other archangels. In the Haggadah, rabbinic sermons from about A.D. [C.E.] 100–500, Michael and Gabriel along with archangels Uriel and Raphael are seen as four angels who surround the throne of God.[5] Other archangels include Uriel, who guards Sheol; Raphael, who is responsible for human spirits; Raguel, the archangel of justice; Michael, the protector of Israel; Gabriel, the guardian of Paradise; and Jeremiel, who guards the souls of the underworld; and Sariel, whose duties are undefined.[6] (The seven archangels, with both the same and different names and functions, are also found in later Christianity and Islam.)

There is also a concept of an angel of death ("*malakh ha-mavet*") that takes the soul from an individual at death, but this angel is not a permanent figure or destroyer of life. Like all angels, the angel of death is a servant of God, and only God has the power to take life. In postbiblical times, however, there came to be a concept of an Angel of Death who acted independently; sometimes, but not always, he was identified as Satan or the fallen angel Samael, but still a created and fallen being.[7]

Another angel that is prominent in the Pseudepigrapha, the *Zohar*, and Jewish mysticism is the angel Metatron. In the *Zohar*, mystical work that first appeared in the thirteenth century and is a key text in Kabbalah, Enoch (Gen. 5:21–24) became Metatron when he was translated (raptured) live into heaven. In heaven Metatron becomes the highest of the angels and ministers near the throne of God.[8]

Kabbalah is a school of mystical thought and interpretation that seeks to understand the relationship between the infinite Creator God and the finite creation of humans and the universe. It has a long and rich history, becoming more widespread in the medieval era and centuries following. It is found primarily in Orthodox and ultra-Orthodox movements as opposed to Conservative and Reform Judaism. Teachings on angels in Kabbalistic thought focus on the struggle between Jacob and the angel (Gen. 32:27) and on the vision of Ezekiel 1 with the four living creatures (cherubim, cf. Ezek. 10:15, 20) and the chariot ("merkabah"). In medieval mysticism, and later among the Hasidim, there is an angel known as Metatron, the highest angel who is charged with the sustenance of humanity and who was popularly believed to be the angel who defends Israel in the heavenly judgment of Yom Kippur.[9]

There are fallen angels in the history of Judaism, and Jewish mysticism distinguishes several categories of angels including ministering angels, corrupting angels, angels of mercy, and angels of judgment.[10] However, the popular idea of guardian angels for individuals is not part of Jewish theology. Concerning angels in contemporary Jewish thought, the *Encyclopedia Judaica* states:

> The modern Jewish attitude to angels tends to regard the traditional references and descriptions as symbolic, poetic, or representing an earlier world-concept. . . . The attitude prevailing among many of the Orthodox is ambiguous. . . . It is only among the small fundamentalistic sections, such as some of the Hasidim as well as the Oriental Jewish communities, that the literal belief in angels, which for so long characterized Jewish thought, is still upheld.[11]

As in Christianity, Jewish angelology has a long and diverse history during which some teachings conform to biblical doctrine and others, based on nonbiblical writings, mysticism, and speculation, depart significantly from it. Grounded in biblical interpretations, there are some parallels and agreement between early Jewish and Christian angelology, but there are also significant differences (for example, the identification of the "Angel of the LORD," who is often understood in Christianity to be the pre-incarnate Jesus Christ).

55. What does Zoroastrianism teach about angels?

Zoroastrianism is a religion that dates to about 1500 B.C. in what was Persia and is now Iran. Some adherents are also found in India and are known as Parsis. Zoroastrianism's founder was a person named Zarathustra who lived in Persia sometime between 1200 and 600 B.C. Zoroastrian theology is dualistic, believing in a good god named Ahura Mazda (also Ohrmazd) and an evil god named Angra Mainyu (also Ahriman). The good god dwells in perfection and light, and the evil god dwells in darkness in eternity. There was a cosmic conflict between the two gods, and Ohrmazd created the heavens and earth and heavenly beings and creatures on earth to assist him in the battle. When Ahriman saw the creation, he tried to destroy it, afflicting it with evil, violence, and suffering.

Zoroastrians believe that the good god will ultimately win, at which time there will be a re-creation of the heavens and earth and all that is good. Zoroastrians consider angels to be very much a part of the cosmic conflict. Angels are divine beings that assist the good god Ahura Mazda with the order and maintenance of the cosmos. There is also another set of subordinate spiritual beings known as the *Amesha Spentas* (the Beneficent Immortals) who are similar to angels and who travel in an entourage with Ahura Mazda. These beings also represent abstract metaphysical concepts and are thought to be the first six emanations of the noncreated god Ahura Mazda; they are referred to as the "divine sparks." In their variously translated names, they are known as Good Thinking (Vohu Manah), Right Mindedness (Armaiti), Harmony (Asha), Power (Xshathra), Wholeness (Haurvatat), and Immortality (Amerretat). They serve as angelic mediators between heaven and earth and are able to grant divine favors including strength, wealth, health, and immortality to individuals on earth.[12]

There is something that is known as a *fravashi*, an entity akin to a guardian angel or guardian spirit in Zoroastrianism. This is also portrayed sometimes as a divine spark, a spiritual component that lives in all of creation, living and not living. Zoroastrians believe that on the fourth day after death, an individual's soul (*urvan*) returns its *fravashi* where its experiences in the physical world are collected for a journey to a bridge. This bridge is guarded by three angelic judges, Mithra, Soroush, and Rashnu, who are the guardians of a person's core values and who determine the eternality of the individual.[13] There is also a tradition of demons or malevolent beings known as *daevas*. In early Zoroastrianism they were considered "wrong gods" or "false gods," but later came to be considered demons.

Because of its great emphasis on a cosmic conflict in the universe, spiritual beings are very much a part of Zoroastrian cosmology and theology. The views are also contrary to the teachings of the Bible and Christianity.

56. What does the Bahá'í Faith teach about angels?

Bahá'í, or more accurately the Bahá'í Faith, is a monotheistic religion founded in the nineteenth century in what was then Persia and now Iran by Bahá'u'lláh (1817–1892). He claimed to be the prophetic fulfillment of Bábism, a religious movement that was an outgrowth of Shí'ism and flourished in Persia from 1844 to 1852. This movement lingered on in exile in the midst of the Ottoman Empire (especially Cyprus) as well as underground. Bahá'u'lláh claimed to be a messenger from God who came to fulfill the expectations of Islam, Christianity, and other major religions of the world.

There are three central principles in Bahá'í teachings and doctrine: the unity of God, the unity of religion, and the unity of humanity. From these doctrines comes the belief that God periodically reveals His will through divine messengers, whose purpose is to transform the character of humanity and develop moral and spiritual qualities within those who respond.

The Bahá'í Faith does not believe in angels and demons as created spiritual beings as in Christianity; they are not seen as a distinct celestial order. Instead, it holds that when such words and concepts appear in the sacred texts of the Bahá'í Faith, they are to be understood metaphorically or allegorically.[14] Also, there is no malevolent figure of Satan or the devil. There is some reference in the Bahá'í Faith to humans transcending to another realm beyond time and space and becoming "angelic" humans and "archangelic Manifestations of God," but such teachings are far removed from biblical thought.

57. What does Sikhism teach about angels?

There is not a developed doctrine of angelology or demonology in Sikhism. Sikhs normally do not believe in the existence of either malevolent or benevolent angels. References to angels or demons in Sikh scriptures and literature are understood to be good or bad qualities in individuals and not spiritual entities. For example, there is a reference in Sikh literature to an angel of death named Azrael, but it is not clear if this is an entity or a concept. Azrael and other angels of death are found also in Islam, Judaism mysticism, and Zoroastrianism. Such angels are not necessarily considered fallen or evil.[15]

58. What do Eastern religions teach about angels?

In general, religions of the East do not have a concept of angels like that found in the monotheistic religions of Judaism, Christianity, and Islam, and their teachings do not agree with biblical truth.

There are strong traditions and ideas of ghosts, spirits, and demons, but the demons are not fallen angels as in Christianity. Many of the religions of the East also have a strong emphasis on ancestor spirits and veneration of ancestors. For example, regarding the memorializing and veneration of spirits, especially in Japan, John K. Nelson writes:

> Unlike Western religious traditions, in which the spirits of the deceased have no lingering engagement with this world, the religious traditions of East Asia and Japan in particular maintain that the spirits of the dead continue to play an active part in the lives of the living. Whoever the deceased may have been in life—a religious leader, a soldier killed in war, the sweetest grandmother in the world—his or her spirit may become angry or vengeful in death; therefore periodic rituals are required long after the funeral to ensure that this does not happen. If the spirits are satisfied, they can become benign and beneficial allies to those who show them the proper respect.[16]

Many of the religions also have complex ideas of demonology, but they lack a concept of a creature such as Satan who is responsible for cosmic evil.

Historically, many of the core ideas in Buddhism are derived from Hinduism, from which Buddhism emerged. In Buddhism there are spiritual entities known as *devas* who are more powerful, longer living, but not immortal, and who are living in a state of contentedness that exceeds that of most humans. They are, however, not the same as angels in religions of the West. It is more accurate to think of ghosts and spirits in Buddhism than angels. They are invisible but can be sensed by humans who have heightened spiritual awareness.[17]

Devas do not require food and are able to fly, but they lose abilities over time. Buddhists believe that *devas* can also have voices capable of being heard by some people. There is a hierarchy of *devas*, and when they die they are transformed into higher or lower levels based upon their karma. They are not omniscient or omnipotent, and they do not serve as spiritual guides for humans.[18] In Buddhism, there are demons that can prevent people from achieving Nirvana, the state of bliss and the extinction of desire. In Japan, where Shinto is prevalent, the concept of *kami* is similar to Buddhism's *devas*. Neither good nor evil, *kami* produce both fear and awe and may be either singular or multiple entities. In Chinese and Japanese folk religions, there are demonlike spirits. Chinese religions know them as *gui-shen* and believe they can be manifested throughout nature. These beings are thought to fear light and, therefore, firecrackers, bonfires, and torches were used to ward off the *gui* (also *guei*).

In Hinduism, *devas* are not angelic-like spirits but gods often in conflict with one another. Things that Christians believe to be ministries of angels are associated with god and goddesses in Hinduism. There are tree spirits, village guardians that are gods and goddesses; there are also beings similar to demons in Hindu mythology known as *asuras*, which are jealous and hostile demons. Additionally, there are serpent demons (*nagas*), a demon of drought also portrayed at times as a serpent or dragon named Ahi, and an archdemon named Kamsa. There are also grotesque beings known as *raksasas* that haunt cemeteries and cause people to act foolishly.[19] As in other religions, the concepts of spiritual beings in Eastern religions is not compatible with biblical teaching.

59. What do indigenous religions teach about angels?

Indigenous religions cover a wide spectrum of belief and practice with many nuances and practices.[20] Indigenous religions, whether in Africa, North America, Central America, South America, Asia, or the Caribbean (some of it transplanted from Africa), do not teach a concept of angels or demons that follows Christianity. Instead, these religions frequently have beliefs in good and evil spirits that are part of nature. Belief in such spirits often stems from a world-view of either animism or polytheism and from a view that does separate the sacred and secular. There is also frequently thought to be a link between the spirit world and one's ancestors , however, not all ancestors are believed to be participants in the spirit world. This is usually reserved for those who lived an exemplary life, empha-sized family, and who did not die a violent death (with the excep-tion of heroic battlefield death).[21]

From a biblical perspective, much of what occurs in indigenous religious is satanic and demonic. To the extent that there are mani-festations of spirits, they are demons. Like any other religion, those things that are not in conformity with the teaching of the Bible are false and are deceptions by Satan, regardless of the sincerity with which they are held (2 Cor. 4:4; 11:14–15).

60. What does Islam teach about angels?

Angels appear frequently in the Qur'an and in Islam. Some of the teaching on angels comes from verses in the Qur'an and other teaching comes from additional writings and tradition. Muslims believe that angels were created from light and that the number of angels is so great that only God knows it. Angels have no gender or offspring. The highest and greatest of the angels is Gabriel (Jibril), whom Muslims believe is the angel through which God transmitted the revelation of the Qur'an to the Prophet Muhammad. Muslims also believe that an angel was used by God to announce to Mary the coming birth of her son, Jesus (Surah 3:45).

Angels are referred to about ninety times in the Qur'an and, among their responsibilities, they are understood to be glorifiers, reciters, guardians, warners, and recorders. Islam classifies cre-ated spiritual beings as angels (*malaikah*), demons/devils (*shayain*), and djinni (genies). "Angels, devils, and jinn, the largest gatherings of spiritual beings that appear in the Qur'an, do not belong to the same cosmic sphere. All they share in common is being invisible;

otherwise, they are differentiated in terms of essence and nature, function, and place in the cosmos."[22]

On some aspects of Islamic angelology, there are clear similarities with the teachings of Judaism and Christianity. From a historical perspective this is understandable, due to the lateness of Islam as a religion and the fact that Muhammad had contact with Jews and Christians who were living in the Arabian Peninsula. As in Christianity and Judaism, Islam teaches that angels worship God and serve as divine messengers. They are thought to accompany Muslims in prayer and also to record the deeds of every person.[23] In addition to Gabriel, other named angels in Islam include Mika'il (Michael), Izra'il, who is responsible for drawing out the souls of the dying, and Israfil, who will sound the trumpet on the day of judgment.[24] (The angel of death is mentioned in Qur'an 32:1, but not named as Izra'il.) There are also the angels Munkar and Nakir, who weigh and question the souls of the dead.

Muslims believe that the angels were created not at one moment in time as in Christianity but over thousands of years. There are also vivid descriptions of some of the angels.[25] Islam also has a mystical tradition, especially in Sufism, with a very elaborate angelology including rituals and symbols.

According to Islamic lore, the djinni or jinn (from which we get *genie*) were created from fire about two thousand years before the creation of Adam. In the same way that Adam was created from dust, jinn are created from smokeless fire by Allah. A genie can become either visible or invisible and assume the forms of animals or humans. They are neutral and either can help or hinder humans but, along with angels and humans, are considered one of the three categories of spiritual beings. Additionally, they can also be manipulated by humans using superior intellect or cunning actions. They are thought to have a complete social structure and free will, and they inhabit a world parallel to humans that can also intersect the human world. They are thought to be capable of traveling at great speeds and often are understood as living in remote areas such as mountains and seas.

The idea of devil or demon is also found in Islam as the idea of accuser and adversary are brought together in the word *shayain*, translated as devil or demon. The word occurs about seventy times in the Qur'an in the singular form, and eighteen times in the plural form.[26]

There is also an evil spiritual being known as a *ghul*, a harmful being who lies in waiting where someone is about to die. In some Muslim folklore (cf. *One Thousand and One Nights*), there is also the activity of the *ghul* plundering graves and feeding on the bodies of the dead. It is from this Arabic term that we have the English word "ghoul," referring either to a grave robber or one who delights in the morbid.

Conclusion

In 1958, C. S. Lewis responded to a woman who had inquired regarding his views on angels. In his response, Lewis declared that angels are "real beings in the actual universe."[1] In this affirmation of the celestial spiritual beings, Lewis was upholding biblical doctrine that has been affirmed by Christians since the first century. Angels are divine emissaries of God used for various ministries in accordance with God's will in the world and in our lives. Angels are a fact of biblical revelation; they are not imaginary, presupposed, or determined by human reasoning. We believe in angels because the Bible tells us about them. But the Bible doesn't tell us everything we would like to know about them. What we can know about angels are things that we understand partially and accurately, but not fully. Some questions will remain unanswered this side of heaven—but they will one day be answered (1 Cor. 13:12).

The writer of Hebrews tells readers, "Do not neglect to show hospitality to strangers, for by this some have entertained angels without knowing it" (13:2). These words stand as a reminder that angels are in our presence, actively ministering even when we do not suspect it. The abundant love, mercy, and grace of God never ceases and the angels are, as Calvin declared "dispensers and administrators of God's beneficence toward us" (*Institutes*, 1.14.6). In our busiest day, our darkest moment, and when life is seemingly carrying us at warp speed, the angels are present, watching, working, and carrying out the will of God as they worship Him. As they learn from us, may we also learn from Scripture and affirm with Christians through the centuries the truths contained in it. The angels are watching!

Notes

Introduction

1. David Van Biema, "Guardian Angels Are Here, Say Most Americans," *Time Magazine*, September 18, 2008, http://www.time .com/time/nation/article/0,8599,1842179,00.html. The entire poll and study is published in Rodney Stark, *What Americans Really Believe* (Waco, TX: Baylor University Press, 2008).

Part 1: Angels, Satan, and Demons in the Bible

1. Ron Rhodes, *Angels Among Us: Separating Fact from Fiction* (Eugene, OR: Harvest House, 2008), 80.
2. Harold W. Hoehner, *Ephesians: An Exegetical Commentary* (Grand Rapids: Baker, 2002), 278–80; 459–60. See also Clinton E. Arnold, *Exegetical Commentary on the New Testament*, vol. 10, *Ephesians* (Grand Rapids: Zondervan, 2010), 111–14.
3. Rhodes, *Angels Among Us*, 95–96.
4. Gustav Davidson, *A Dictionary of Angels Including the Fallen Angels* (New York: Free Press, 1967), 51.
5. C. Fred Dickason, *Angels, Elect & Evil*, rev. and exp. (Chicago: Moody Press, 1995), 66.
6. It is, however, also possible that the reference to "feet" here is a Hebrew euphemism for genitals as in Ruth 3:4 and elsewhere.

See Robert L. Hubbard, *The Book of Ruth*, NICOT (Grand Rapids: Eerdmans, 1988), 203. Angels do not procreate and therefore, if in this passage there is a sexual euphemism, it would be because at times angels take on the appearance of human form.

7. Robert L. Thomas, *Revelation 1–7: An Exegetical Commentary* (Chicago: Moody Press, 1992), 358. See also Dickason, *Angels: Elect and Evil*, 69.

8. Rhodes, *Angels Among Us*, 131.

9. The Hebrew word *shin'an* translated in the NASB as "thousands upon thousands" and elsewhere as "countless" or "immeasurable" is used only this one time in the Bible, making its exact translation difficult.

10. Rhodes, *Angels Among Us*, 91.

11. Thomas Aquinas, *Summa Theologica* 1.50.3.

12. Thomas, *Revelation 1–7*, 403–4.

13. Craig S. Keener, *The IVP Bible Background Commentary* (Downers Grove, IL: InterVarsity Press, 1993), 779.

14. For a detailed discussion, see John F. Walvoord, *Jesus Christ Our Lord* (Chicago: Moody Press, 1969), 44–46, 52–42. See also, Rhodes, *Angels Among Us*, 117–28.

15. See Dickason, *Angels, Elect & Evil*, 95–106; and Rhodes, *Angels Among Us*, 139–82. See also Charles C. Ryrie, *Basic Theology* (Wheaton, IL: Victor Books, 1986), 131–33.

16. For an overview of biblical prophecy and events yet to be fulfilled, see in this same series, Timothy J. Demy and Thomas Ice, *Answers to Common Questions About the End Times*.

17. Dickason, *Angels, Elect & Evil*, 102–6.

18. Darrell L. Bock, *Luke 9:51–24:53*, Baker Exegetical Commentary on the New Testament (Grand Rapids: Baker, 1996), 1368.

19. The Hebrew equivalent of Apollyon, meaning "destroyer."

20. According to Rev. 9:11, the Greek word means "destroyer."

21. The term also is found as Beelzebub (a Philistine deity), a name possibly meaning "lord of flies."

22. Devil, a popular name for the enemy of God and man, means a "slanderer."

23. See Charles Lee Feinberg, *The Prophecy of Ezekiel: The Glory of the Lord* (Chicago: Moody Press, 1969), 158–64.

24. See the authors' *Answers to Common Questions About Jesus*, for an explanation of why the biblical text in Matt. 24:36 says the Son does not know the time of His own coming.

25. In this verse the NASB translates the Hebrew word *helel*, "star of the morning," but the Latin Vulgate translates it by the Latin term *lucifer*. The King James Version, however, makes the Hebrew word a name (Lucifer), after the Latin, rather than translating it.

26. See Bock, *Luke 9:51–24:53*, 1006 n. 38.

27. For a brief discussion of the options for identifying this figure, see Ryrie, *Basic Theology*, 141–42.

28. For an extended analysis of these habitations, see Arnold G. Fruchtenbaum, "The Six Abodes of Satan," in *Footsteps of the Messiah*, rev. ed. (Tustin, CA: Ariel Ministries, 2003), 551–71.

29. Ibid., 556–64.

30. Satan will be bound during the millennium because God is demonstrating during that period that with every external source of temptation removed, humanity is still a rebel against God in their hearts and in need of the grace of God. Satan is released at the end of the millennium to draw out for final judgment those who in the course of Christ's reign have been secret rebels, and to finally judge Satan.

31. Ryrie, *Basic Theology*, 151.

32. Ibid.

33. For more on this time period, see in this same series, Demy and Ice, *Answers to Common Questions About the End Times*, 59–98.

34. Fruchtenbaum, *Footsteps of the Messiah*, 246–47.

35. John F. Walvoord, *Major Bible Prophecies* (Grand Rapids: Zondervan, 1991), 404.

36. Wayne Grudem, *Systematic Theology: An Introduction to Biblical Doctrine* (Grand Rapids: Zondervan, 1994), 413 n. 4.

37. For an extensive study on these ideas, see John C. Poirier, *Tongues of Angels: The Concept of Angelic Languages in Classical Jewish & Christian Texts* (Tübingen: Mohr Siebeck, 2010).

38. A question and consideration of biblical theology comes in here—how is the phrase used at the earlier period of biblical history versus later periods like the Psalms and Minor Prophets? Job and Genesis refer to the antediluvian or patriarchal periods. This shows that words are not always used to mean the same thing throughout their history. Meanings may or may not change, and it is important for the student of the Bible to carefully study usage and be aware of the possibility of lexical changes throughout centuries of usage.

39. There is much literature and commentary on the "sons of God" interpretations. In addition to the views of the sons of God being angels or despotic rulers, some interpreters have understood them to be from the line of Seth so that the verse is stating that there was intermarriage between the lines of Adam— godly Sethites and ungodly Caninites. For an overview, see Allen P. Ross, *Creation & Blessing: A Guide to the Study and Exposition of Genesis* (Grand Rapids: Baker, 1988), 181–83; Arnold Fruchtenbaum, *The Book of Genesis* (San Antonio: Ariel Ministries, 2009), 143–52; and Arnold Fruchtenbaum, *Messianic Christology* (Tustin, CA: Ariel Ministries, 1998), 118–22. In the pages of the latter work, Fruchtenbaum also addresses 2 Peter 2:4–5 and Jude 6–7.

40. For an extended study of this question and passage, see Wayne Grudem, "Christ Preaching Through Noah: 1 Peter 3:19–20 in Light of Dominant Themes in Jewish Literature," *Trinity Journal* 7:2 (Fall 1986): 3–31. See also Karen H. Jobes, *1 Peter* (Grand Rapids: Baker, 2005), 243–51.

41. The phrase "He descended into hell" is first mentioned in a form of the creed in 359 but then not used until later. It was

not part of the earliest forms on the creed. Wayne Grudem writes:

> It is surprising to find that the phrase "He descended into hell" was not found in any of the early versions of the Creed (in the versions used in Rome, in the rest of Italy, in Africa) until it appeared in one of two versions from Rufinus in A.D. 390. Then it is not included again in any version of the Creed until 650. Moreover Rufinus, the only person who includes it before 650, did not think that it meant that Christ descended into hell but understood the phrase simply to mean that Christ was "buried." In other words, he took it to mean that Christ "descended into the grave." (The Greek form has *hadēs*, which can mean just "grave," not *geenna*, "hell, place of punishment.") We should also note that the phrase only appears in one of the two versions of the Creed that we have from Rufinus. It was not in the Roman form of the Creed that he preserved.
>
> But this means that until A.D. 650 no version of the Creed included this phrase with the intention of saying that Christ "descended into hell." The only version to include the phrase before 650 gives it a different meaning. Wayne Grudem, "He Did Not Descend into Hell: A Plea for Following Scripture Instead of the Apostles' Creed," *Journal of the Evangelical Theological Society* 34:1 (March 1991): 103–6.

42. For a presentation supporting this interpretation, see Arnold G. Fruchtenbaum, *Hebrews, James, I & II Peter, Jude*, Ariel's Bible Commentary (Tustin, CA: Ariel Ministries, 2005), 360–63.

43. The grammar of the Greek is plain. The word "angels" refers grammatically to the sexual immortality, viz. "in the same way." The Sodomites followed after "strange" flesh and so did the angels.

44. See Fruchtenbaum, *Hebrews, James, I & II Peter, Jude,* 432–34; and Gene L. Green, *Jude & 2 Peter* (Grand Rapids: Baker, 2008), 66–73.

45. For an exposition, see Green, *Jude & 2 Peter,* 79–84.

Part 2: Angels and Demons in Christian History and Theology

1. See Maxwell J. Davidson, *Angels at Qumran: A Comparative Study of 1 Enoch 1–36, 72–108 and Sectarian Writings from Qumran* (Sheffield: JSOT Press, 1992).

2. See Andy M. Reimer, "Rescuing the Fallen Angels: The Case of the Disappearing Angels at Qumran," *Dead Sea Discoveries* 7:3 (2000): 334–53.

3. R. M. M. Tuschling, *Angels & Orthodoxy: A Study in Their Development in Syria and Palestine from the Qumran Texts to Ephrem the Syrian* (Tübingen: Mohr Siebeck, 2007), 136.

4. The history of the *Book of Enoch* is a large field of study with many diverse views. On *Beowulf* and *Paradise Lost,* respectively, see R. E. Kaske, "*Beowulf* and the Book of Enoch," *Speculum* XLVI:3 (July 1971): 421–31; Grant McColley, "The *Book of Enoch* and *Paradise Lost,*" *Harvard Theological Review* 31:1 (Jan. 1938): 21–39; and Arnold Williams, "Milton and the *Book of Enoch*: An Alternative Hypothesis," *Harvard Theological Review* 33:4 (Oct. 1940): 291–99.

5. *Book of Enoch* 8.1. Interestingly, this story also sounds like that of Prometheus in Greek mythology.

6. Jaroslav Pelikan, *The Emergence of the Catholic Tradition (100–600),* vol. 1 of *The Christian Tradition: A History of the Development of Doctrine* (Chicago: University of Chicago Press, 1971), 182–84.

7. Ibid., 151.

8. Origen, *Princ.* 1.7.1; *Comm. Matt.* 17.2. See also Tuschling, *Angels & Orthodoxy,* 137–39.

9. Ibid., 133–34.

10. For a summary of the Fathers and references, see Gerald L. Bray and Thomas C. Oden, eds., *We Believe in One God: Ancient Christian Doctrine*, vol. 1 (Downers Grove, IL: InterVarsity Press, 2009), 128–49; and "Angels," in *New Catholic Encyclopedia*, 2nd ed., 1:418–21.

11. Jean Daniélou, *The Angels & Their Mission* (Manchester, NH: Sophia Institute Press, repr. ed., 2009), 16–22. See also Michael S. Heiser, "Deuteronomy 32:8 and the Sons of God," *Bibliotheca Sacra* 158:629 (Jan.–Mar. 2001): 52–74. See also David E. Stevens, "Daniel 10 and the Notion of Territorial Spirits," *Bibliotheca Sacra* 157:628 (Oct.–Dec. 2000): 410–31. In the latter article, there is a strong argument that use of the word "prince" in Daniel 10:13, 20 is a reference to a demon and that the influence exerted by them in the context is sociopolitical and personal and not territorial, thus invalidating interpretation some contemporary proponents of the idea of "territorial spirits."

12. Ibid., 18.

13. See Richard Bauckham, "The Fall of the Angels as the Source of Philosophy in Hermias and Clement of Alexandria," *Vigiliae Christianae* 39:4 (December 1985): 313–30.

14. Pelikan, *Emergence of the Catholic Tradition (100–600)*, 134–35.

15. Daniélou, *Angels & Their Mission*, 75–91.

16. Ibid., 88.

17. F. X. Murphy, "Pseudo-Dionysius," in *New Catholic Encyclopedia*, 2nd ed., vol. 11 (Detroit and Washington, DC: Gale Group and Catholic University of America, 2003), 800–801.

18. *De Colesti Hierarchia* 6.7–9, http://www.ccel.org/ccel/pearse/morefathers/files/areopagite_13_heavenly_hierarchy.htm#c6.

19. Frederick Van Fleteren, "Angels," in *Augustine Through the Ages*, ed. Allan D. Fitzgerald (Grand Rapids: Eerdmans, 1999), 21.

20. David Keck, *Angels and Angelology in the Middle Ages* (New York: Oxford University Press, 1998), 3.

21. Ibid., 6. For a comprehensive study of Aquinas and angels, see James Collins, *The Thomistic Philosophy of the Angels* (Washington, DC: Catholic University of America Press, 1947). On the revival of Aristotle and its effects on theology, see Richard E. Rubenstein, *Aristotle's Children: How Christians, Muslims, Jews Rediscovered Ancient Wisdom and Illuminated the Middle Ages* (Orlando, FL: Harcourt Books, 2003).

22. Ibid., 19.

23. Ibid., 13.

24. Ibid., 7.

25. Ibid., 16.

26. On the study of the Bible in this era, see Beryl Smalley, *The Study of the Bible in the Middle Ages* (Notre Dame: University of Notre Dame Press, 1964).

27. Cf. Keck, *Angels and Angelology in the Middle Ages*, 75–92.

28. Among the things Lombard addressed were: the creation of angels, the precise timing of the creation of angels, location of the creation of angels, qualities of angels at creation, fall and confirmation of angels, location and powers of fallen angels, the attributes of angels and demons (cognitive, moral, and physical), corporeality of angels and demons, angelic hierarchies, ministries of angels to humans, and guardian angels.

29. Ibid., 90.

30. For example, "Q. 50. Of the Substance of the Angels Absolutely Considered" is divided into the following questions with a detailed response: (1) Whether there is any entirely spiritual creature, altogether incorporeal? (2) Supposing that an angel is such, we ask whether it is composed of matter and form? (3) We ask concerning their number. (4) Of their difference from each other. (5) Of their immortality or incorruptibility. *Summa theologica 1.50*, http://www.ccel.org/a/aquinas/summa/FP/FP050.html#FPQ50OUTP1.

31. Keck, *Angels and Angelology in the Middle Ages*, 161–65.

32. For an introduction to the vast field of medieval eschatology,

see Bernard McGinn, *Visions of the End: Apocalyptic Traditions in the Middle Ages* (New York: Cornell University Press, 1974). For Joachim of Fiore specifically, see Marjorie Reeves, *Joachim of Fiore and the Prophetic Future* (Stroud, UK: Sutton Publishing, 1999) and Marjorie Reeves, *The Influence of Prophecy in the Late Middle Ages* (Notre Dame: University of Notre Dame Press, 1994).

33. On medieval views on Satan, see Jeffrey Burton Russell, *Lucifer: The Devil in the Middle Ages* (Ithaca, NY: Cornell University Press, 1984). On magic and demonology in the era, see Valerie I. J. Flint, *The Rise of Magic in Early Medieval Europe* (Princeton: Princeton University Press, 1994), esp. 101–7, 146–84. Also see Euan Cameron, *Enchanted Europe: Superstition, Reason, and Religion, 1250–1750* (New York: Oxford University Press, 2010), esp. 89–118.

34. Keck, *Angels and Angelology in the Middle Ages,* 212.

35. Joad Raymond, *Milton's Angels: The Early Modern Imagination* (Oxford: Oxford University Press, 2010), 32.

36. Cited by ibid. Also on angels in Renaissance thought, see Bruce Gordon, "The Renaissance Angel," in *Angels in the Early Modern World,* ed. by Peter Marshall and Alexandra Walsham (Cambridge: Cambridge University Press, 2006), 41–63.

37. Peter Marshall and Alexandra Walsham, "Migrations of Angels in the Early Modern World," in *Angels in the Early Modern World*, ed. by Peter Marshall and Alexandra Walsham (Cambridge: Cambridge University Press, 2006), 13.

38. On the history of the doctrine of Satan in the Reformation, see Jeffrey Burton Russell, *Mephistopheles: The Devil in the Modern World* (Ithaca, NY: Cornell University Press, 1986), 25–76.

39. Marshall and Walsham, "Migrations of Angels," 14.

40. Raymond, *Milton's Angels,* 35.

41. Ibid.

42. Philip M. Soergel, "Luther on Angels," in *Angels in the Early*

Modern World, ed. by Peter Marshall and Alexandra Walsham (Cambridge: Cambridge University Press, 2006), 67. Soergel's essay provides an excellent overview of Luther's angelology.

43. Raymond, *Milton's Angels,* 36.

44. See Alexandra Walsham, "Angels and Idols in England's Long Reformation," in *Angels in the Early Modern World*, ed. by Peter Marshall and Alexandra Walsham (Cambridge: Cambridge University Press, 2006), 134–67.

45. Calvin, *Institutes of the Christian Religion*, 1.14.6 (McNeill/ Battles ed. 1:167).

46. Raymond, *Milton's Angels,* 33.

47. Calvin, *Institutes of the Christian Religion,* 1.14.4.

48. Raymond, *Milton's Angels,* 37.

49. Soergel, "Luther on Angels," 66.

50. This may well be so because God can act in time through theophany or through angelic beings but cannot exist in time or be bound down to finite events in time, such as communication apart from these intermediaries.

51. Marshall and Walsham, "Migrations of Angels," 14–15.

52. Peter Kreeft, *Angels (and Demons)* (San Francisco: Ignatius Press, 1995), 70–71.

53. Helen S. Lang, *Aristotle's Physics and Its Medieval Varieties* (Albany, NY: State University of New York Press, 1992), 284.

54. Cited in George Macdonald Ross, "Angels," *Philosophy* 60:234 (October 1985): 495 n. 2 (translation ours).

55. William Chillingworth, Preface to *The Religion of Protestants a Safe Way to Salvation* (Oxford: Leonard Lichfield, 1638), n.p., at numerated paragraph 19.

56. Richard Baxter, *The Reasons of the Christian Religion* (London: 1667), 530. It can be found at Google Books, http://books .google.com.

57. David Albert Jones, *Angels: A History* (Oxford: Oxford University Press, 2010), 18–19.

58. Ibid., 21–22.

59. See, for example, Peter Marshall, "Angels Around the Death-bed: Variations on a Theme in the English Art of Dying," in *Angels in the Early Modern World*, ed. Peter Marshall and Alexandra Walsham (Cambridge: Cambridge University Press, 2006), 83–103.

60. See Dov Noy, "Angel of Death," *Encyclopedia Judaica*, 2nd ed., 2:147–50.

61. Raymond, *Milton's Angels*, 384.

62. See Feisal G. Mohamed, *In the Anteroom of Divinity: The Reformation of the Angels from Colet to Milton* (Toronto: University of Toronto Press, 2008).

63. Robert H. West, "Milton's Angelological Heresies," *Journal of the History of Ideas* 14:1 (January 1953): 116. See also West's "The Names of Milton's Angels," *Studies in Philology* 47:2 (April 1950): 211–23.

64. Diane McColley, "Angel," in David Lyle Jeffrey, ed., *A Dictionary of Biblical Tradition in English Literature* (Grand Rapids: Eerdmans, 1992), 40. See also P. L. Carver, "The Angels in *Paradise Lost*," *Review of English Studies* 16:64 (Oct. 1940): 415–31.

Part 3: Angels, Satan, and Demons in the World Today

1. Darrell L. Bock, *Luke 9:51–24:53* (Madison, WI: InterVarsity Press, 1994), 1368 n. 15.

2. For a fuller discussion, see Robert Dean, Jr. and Thomas Ice, *What the Bible Teaches About Spiritual Warfare* (Grand Rapids: Kregel, 2000), 134–47.

3. See Ron Rhodes, *Angels Among Us: Separating Fact from Fiction* (Eugene, OR: Harvest House, 2008), 204–5.

4. John F. Walvoord, *Daniel: The Key to Prophetic Revelation* (Chicago: Moody Press, 1971), 245–51; and Stephen R. Miller, *Daniel*, The New American Commentary, vol. 18 (Nashville: Broadman & Holman, 1994), 283–87.

5. Harold Hoehner, *Ephesians* (Grand Rapids: Baker, 2002), 831.

6. Ibid., 147.

7. On the early history of the doctrine of guardian angels in Christianity, see Roman Catholic theologian Jean Daniélou, *The Angels & Their Mission* (Manchester, NH: Sophia Institute Press, 2009), 75–91.

8. Calvin, *Institutes of the Christian Religion*, 1.14.6.

9. Some groups such as Latter-day Saints erroneously believe that there are some angels who were previously human (for example, Michael was Adam and Gabriel was Noah). On their belief, see "The Guide to the Scriptures" under "Angels" at the LDS website at http://lds.org/scriptures/gs/angels?lang=eng and "Is the Angel Moroni a Resurrected Being?" at http://lds.about.com/cs/basicbeliefs/f/angels.htm.

10. The same is true for those who are mentally handicapped to the extent that they apparently do not have the capacity and understanding to believe. For more on the very difficult emotional, pastoral, and theological issues of the death of the unborn, infants, and children, as well as those with diminished mental capacities, see in this same series Demy and Ice, *Answers to Common Questions About Heaven & Eternity*, 47–49. See also Robert P. Lightner, *Safe in the Arms of Jesus: God's Provision for the Death of Those Who Cannot Believe* (Grand Rapids: Kregel, 2000) and John MacArthur, *Safe in the Arms of God: Truth from Heaven About the Death of a Child* (Nashville: Thomas Nelson, 2003).

11. C. Fred Dickason, *Angels: Elect & Evil* (Chicago: Moody Press, 1995), 13–14.

12. J. Dwight Pentecost, *Your Adversary the Devil* (Grand Rapids: Zondervan, 1969), 130.

Part 4: Angels, Satan, and Demons in World Religions

1. For an overview, see "Angels and Angelology," in *Encyclopedia Judaica*, vol. 2, 2nd ed. (New York: Macmillan Reference,

2007), 150–61. See also Morris B. Margolies, *A Gathering of Angels: Angels in Jewish Life and Literature* (New York: Ballantine Books, 1994).

2. Not all Jewish commentators hold that there was a denial of angels by the Sadducees, arguing that Acts 23:8 is the only evidence of this view and is unclear. For this, see Bernard J. Bamberger, "The Sadducees and the Belief in Angels," *Journal of Biblical Literature* 82:4 (Dec. 1963): 433–35. See also "Angels and Angelology," in *Encyclopedia Judaica*, 2nd ed., 153.

3. Harold B. Kuhn, "The Angelology of the Noncanonical Jewish Apocalypses," *Journal of Biblical Literature* 67:3 (Sept. 1948): 219–20.

4. David Wolpe, "Angels in Jewish Tradition," at http://www.beliefnet.com/Faiths/Judaism/2002/04/Angels-In-Jewish-Tradition.aspx?p=2.

5. "Michael and Gabriel," *Encyclopedia Judaica*, 2nd ed., vol. 14 (New York: Macmillan Reference, 2007), 168.

6. "Angels and Angelology," in *Encyclopedia Judaica*, 2:153.

7. "Angel of Death," in *Encyclopedia Judaica*, 2:148.

8. Margolies, *Gathering of Angels,* 80–81.

9. Gustav Davidson, *A Dictionary of Angels: Including the Fallen Angels* (New York: Free Press, 1967), 192–93. See also Andrea Piras, "Angels," in *Encyclopedia of Religion*, 2nd ed., 345–46.

10. "Angels and Angelology," in *Encyclopedia Judaica*, 2:159.

11. Ibid., 161.

12. Andrea Piras, "Angels, Zoroastrianism," in *Encyclopedia of Religion*, 2nd ed., vol. 1 (New York: Macmillan Reference, 2005), 344.

13. "After Life and Funeral Customs," at www.heritageinstitute.com/zoroastrianism/death/index.htm.

14. Peter Smith, *A Concise Encyclopedia of the Bahá'í Faith* (Oxford: Oneworld Publications, 2000), 304.

15. Davidson, *Dictionary of Angels,* 26.

16. John K. Nelson, "Japanese Traditions," in *World Religions: Eastern Traditions,* 3rd ed., ed. Willard G. Oxtoby and Roy C. Amore (New York: Oxford University Press, 2010), 352–53.

17. See Peter Masefield, "Ghosts and Spirits," in *Encyclopedia of Buddhism,* ed. Robert E. Buswell Jr. (New York: Macmillan, 2004), 1:309–10.

18. "Angels in Buddhism," in *Wisdom Quarterly: American Buddhist Journal* (electronic), January 2010 at http://wisdomquar terly.blogspot.com/2010/01/angels-in-buddhism.html.

19. "Yaksas and Raksasas," at http://www.harekrsna.com/philos ophy/associates/demons/classes/yaksas.htm.

20. For an overview of indigenous religions, see Christopher Partridge, ed., *Introduction to World Religions* (Minneapolis: Fortress Press, 2005), 100–133. See also charts 86–101 in H. Wayne House, *Charts of World Religions* (Grand Rapids: Zondervan, 2006).

21. Molefi Kete Asante, "Ancestors," in *Encyclopedia of African Religion,* ed. Molefi Kete Asante and Ama Mazama (Los Angeles: Sage Publications, 2009), 1:45–46.

22. Stefania Cunial, "Spiritual Beings," in *Encyclopedia of the Qur'an,* ed. Jane Dammen McAuliffe (Leiden: Brill, 2006), 5:118. See also Jacqueline Chabbi, "Jinn," *Encyclopedia of the Qur'an,* 3:43–49.

23. Peter G. Riddell, [Islamic] "Beliefs," in *Introduction to World Religions,* ed. Christopher Partridge (Minneapolis: Fortress Press, 2005), 373–74.

24. Ibid., 374.

25. Peter Lamborn Wilson, "Angels," in *Encyclopedia of Islam and the Muslim World,* ed. Richard C. Martin (New York: Macmillan, 2004), 1:49.

26. Andrew Rippin, "Devil," in *Encyclopedia of the Qur'an,* 1:524.

Conclusion

1. C. S. Lewis, "Letter to Mrs Hook, 29 Dec 1958," in *Collected Letters of C. S. Lewis, Vol. III Narnia, Cambridge, and Joy 1950–1963*, ed. Walter Hooper (San Francisco: HarperCollins, 2007), 1005.

Recommended Reading

Adler, Joseph A. *Chinese Religious Traditions.* Upper Saddle River, NJ: Prentice Hall, 2002.

Adler, Mortimer J. *The Angels and Us.* New York: Collier Books, 1982.

Ankerberg, John, and John Weldon. *The Facts on Angels.* Eugene, OR: Harvest House, 1995.

Arnold, Clinton E. *Exegetical Commentary on the New Testament, vol. 10, Ephesians.* Grand Rapids: Zondervan, 2010.

Asante, Molefi Kete, and Ama Mazama, eds. *Encyclopedia of African Religion.* 2 vols. Los Angeles: Sage Publications, 2009.

Bamberger, Bernard J. "The Sadducees and the Belief in Angels." *Journal of Biblical Literature* 82:4 (December 1963): 433–35.

Bildhauer, Bettina, and Robert Mills, eds. *The Monstrous Middle Ages.* Cardiff: University of Wales Press, 2003.

Bock, Darrell L. *Luke 9:51—24:53, Baker Exegetical Commentary on the New Testament.* Grand Rapids: Baker, 1996.

Bulgakov, Sergius. *Jacob's Ladder: On Angels.* Translated by Thomas Allan Smith. Grand Rapids: Eerdmans, 2010.

Buswell, Robert E., Jr., ed. *Encyclopedia of Buddhism.* 2 vols. New York: Macmillan, 2004.

Calvin, John. *Institutes of the Christian Religion.* 2 vols. Edited by John T. McNeill. Translated and indexed by Ford Lewis Battles. Philadelphia: Westminster Press, 1960.

Cameron, Euan. *Enchanted Europe: Superstition, Reason, and Religion, 1250–1750*. New York: Oxford University Press, 2010.

Carver, P. L. "The Angels in *Paradise Lost.*" *The Review of English Studies* 16:64 (October 1940): 415–31.

Chillingworth, William. *The Religion of Protestants a Safe Way to Salvation*. Oxford: Leonard Lichfield, 1638.

Colish, Marcia L. "Early Scholastic Angelology." *Reserches de Théologie ancienne et médiévale* 62 (1995): 80–109.

Collins, James. *The Thomistic Philosophy of the Angels*. Washington, DC: Catholic University of America Press, 1947.

Daniélou, Jean. *The Angels & Their Mission*. Manchester, NH: Sophia Institute Press, reprint ed., 2009.

Davidson, Gustav. *A Dictionary of Angels Including the Fallen Angels*. New York: Free Press, 1967.

Davidson, Maxwell J. *Angels at Qumran: A Comparative Study of 1 Enoch 1–36, 72–108 and Sectarian Writings from Qumran*. Sheffield: JSOT Press, 1992.

Dean, Robert, Jr., and Thomas Ice. *What the Bible Teaches About Spiritual Warfare*. Grand Rapids: Kregel, 2000.

Demy, Timothy J., and Thomas Ice. *Answers to Common Questions About the End Times*. Grand Rapids: Kregel, 2011.

_____. *Answers to Common Questions About Heaven & Eternity*. Grand Rapids: Kregel, 2011.

Dickason, C. Fred. *Angels, Elect & Evil*. Chicago: Moody Press, 1995.

Encyclopedia Judaica 2nd ed. 22 vols. New York: Macmillan Reference, 2007.

Evans, Tony. *The Truth About Angels and Demons*. Chicago: Moody Press, 2005.

Feinberg, Charles Lee. *The Prophecy of Ezekiel: The Glory of the Lord*. Chicago: Moody Press, 1969.

Fitzgerald, Allan D., ed. *Augustine Through the Ages: An Encyclopedia*. Grand Rapids: Eerdmans, 1999.

Flint, Valerie I. J. *The Rise of Magic in Early Medieval Europe*. Princeton: Princeton University Press, 1994.

Fruchtenbaum, Arnold G. *The Book of Genesis.* San Antonio: Ariel Ministries, 2009.

————. *The Footsteps of the Messiah.* Rev. ed. Tustin, CA: Ariel Ministries, 2003.

————. *Hebrews, James, I & II Peter, Jude.* Tustin, CA: Ariel Ministries, 2005.

————. *Messianic Christology.* Tustin, CA: Ariel Ministries, 1998.

Garrett, Susan R. *No Ordinary Angel: Celestial Spirits and Claims About Jesus.* New Haven: Yale University Press, 2008.

Green, Gene. L. *Jude & 2 Peter.* Grand Rapids: Baker, 2008.

Grudem, Wayne. "Christ Preaching Through Noah: 1 Peter 3:19–20 in Light of Dominant Themes in Jewish Literature." *Trinity Journal* 7:2 (Fall 1986): 3–31.

————. "He Did Not Descend into Hell: A Plea for Following Scripture Instead of the Apostles' Creed." *Journal of the Evangelical Theological Society* 34:1 (March 1991): 103–13.

————. *Systematic Theology: An Introduction to Biblical Doctrine.* Grand Rapids: Zondervan, 1994.

Heiser, Michael S. "Deuteronomy 32:8 and the Sons of God." *Bibliotheca Sacra* 158:629 (Jan.–Mar. 2001): 52–74.

Hoehner, Harold W. *Ephesians: An Exegetical Commentary.* Grand Rapids: Baker Academic, 2002.

House, H. Wayne. *Charts of World Religions.* Grand Rapids: Zondervan, 2006.

Hubbard, Robert L. *The Book of Ruth.* Grand Rapids: Eerdmans, 1988.

Isaacs, Ronald. *Ascending Jacob's Ladder: Jewish Views of Angels, Demons, and Evil Spirits.* Lanham, MD: Rowman & Littlefield, 1998.

Jeffrey, David Lyle, ed. *A Dictionary of Biblical Tradition in English Literature.* Grand Rapids: Eerdmans, 1992.

Jeremiah, David. *Angels.* Colorado Springs: Multnomah, 2006.

Jobes, Karen H. *1 Peter.* Grand Rapids: Baker, 2005.

Jones, David Albert. *Angels: A History.* Oxford: Oxford University Press, 2010.

Kaske, R. E. "*Beowulf* and the *Book of Enoch*." *Speculum* XLVI:3 (July 1971): 421–31.

Keck, David. *Angels and Angelology in the Middle Ages.* New York: Oxford University Press, 1998.

Keener, Craig S. *The IVP Bible Background Commentary.* Downers Grove, IL: InterVarsity Press, 1993.

Kreeft, Peter. *Angels (and Demons).* San Francisco: Ignatius Press, 1995.

Kuhn, Harold B. "The Angelology of the Noncanonical Jewish Apocalypses." *Journal of Biblical Literature* 67:3 (September 1948): 217–32.

Lang, Helen S. *Aristotle's Physics and Its Medieval Varieties.* Albany, NY: State University of New York Press, 1992.

Lightner, Robert P. *Safe in the Arms of Jesus: God's Provision for the Death of Those Who Cannot Believe.* Grand Rapids: Kregel, 2000.

Lutzer, Erwin W. *The Serpent of Paradise.* Chicago: Moody Press, 1996.

MacArthur, John. *Safe in the Arms of God: Truth from Heaven About the Death of a Child.* Nashville: Thomas Nelson, 2003.

Margolies, Morris B. *A Gathering of Angels: Angels in Jewish Life and Literature.* New York: Ballantine, 1994.

Marshall, Peter, and Alexandra Walsham, eds. *Angels in the Early Modern World.* Cambridge: Cambridge University Press, 2006.

Martin, Richard C., ed. *Encyclopedia of Islam and the Muslim World.* 2 vols. New York: Macmillan, 2004.

McAuliffe, Jane Dammen, ed. *Encyclopedia of the Qur'an.* 5 vols. Leiden: Brill, 2006.

McColley, Grant. "The *Book of Enoch* and *Paradise Lost*." *Harvard Theological Review* 31:1 (January 1938): 21–39.

McGinn, Bernard. *Visions of the End: Apocalyptic Traditions in the Middle Ages.* New York: Cornell University Press, 1974.

Miller, Stephen R. *Daniel.* The New American Commentary. Nashville: Broadman & Holman, 1994.

Mohamed, Feisal G. *In the Anteroom of Divinity: The Reformation of the Angels from Colet to Milton.* Toronto: University of Toronto Press, 2008.

Montgomery, John Warwick. *Principalities and Powers.* Minneapolis: Bethany House, 1981.

Mounce, William D., ed. *Mounce's Complete Expository Dictionary of Old & New Testament Words.* Grand Rapids: Zondervan, 2006.

New Catholic Encyclopedia. 2nd ed. 15 vols. Detroit and Washington, DC: Gale Group and The Catholic University of America, 2003.

Oden, Thomas C., ed. *Ancient Christian Doctrine.* 5 vols. Downers Grove, IL: InterVarsity Press, 2009–10.

Oxtby, Willard G., and Amir Hussain, eds. *World Religions: Western Traditions.* 3rd ed. New York: Oxford University Press, 2011.

Oxtoby, Willard G., and Roy C. Amore, eds. *World Religions: Eastern Traditions.* 3rd ed. New York: Oxford University Press, 2010.

Partridge, Christopher, ed. *Introduction to World Religions.* Minneapolis: Fortress Press, 2005.

Pelikan, Jaroslav. *The Christian Tradition: A History of the Development of Doctrine.* 5 vols. Chicago: University of Chicago Press, 1971–91.

Pentecost, J. Dwight. *Your Adversary the Devil.* Grand Rapids: Zondervan, 1969.

Poirier, John C. *Tongues of Angels: The Concept of Angelic Languages in Classical Jewish & Christian Texts.* Tübingen: Mohr Siebeck, 2010.

Raymond, Joad. *Milton's Angels: The Early-Modern Imagination.* Oxford: Oxford University Press, 2010.

_____. "Protestant Culture: Milton's Angels." *History Today* 60:12

(November 2010), at http://www.historytoday.com/joad-ray
          mond/protestant-culture-miltons-angels.

Reeves, Marjorie. *The Influence of Prophecy in the Late Middle Ages.*
          Notre Dame: University of Notre Dame Press, 1994.

_____. *Joachim of Fiore and the Prophetic Future.* Stroud (UK):
          Sutton Publishing, 1999.

Rhodes, Ron. *Angels Among Us.* Eugene, OR: Harvest House, 2008.

Ross, Allen P. *Creation & Blessing: A Guide to the Study and
          Exposition of Genesis.* Grand Rapids: Baker, 1988.

Ross, George Macdonald. "Angels." *Philosophy* 60:234 (October
          1985): 495–511.

Rubenstein, Richard E. *Aristotle's Children: How Christians, Muslims,
          Jews Rediscovered Ancient Wisdom and Illuminated the
          Middle Ages.* Orlando, FL: Harcourt Books, 2003.

Russell, Jeffrey Burton. *Lucifer: The Devil in the Middle Ages.* Ithaca,
          NY: Cornell University Press, 1984.

_____. *Mephistopheles: The Devil in the Modern World.* Ithaca,
          NY: Cornell University Press, 1986.

_____. *Satan: The Early Christian Tradition.* Ithaca, NY: Cornell
          University Press, 1981.

Ryrie, Charles C. *Basic Theology.* Wheaton, IL: Victor Books, 1986.

Scribner, Robert W. "The Reformation, Popular Magic, and the
          'Disenchantment of the World.'" *Journal of Interdisciplin-
          ary History* 23:3, Religion and History (Winter 1993):
          475–94.

Smalley, Beryl. *The Study of the Bible in the Middle Ages.* Notre
          Dame: University of Notre Dame Press, 1964.

Smith, Peter. *A Concise Encyclopedia of the Bahá'í Faith.* Oxford:
          Oneworld Publications, 2000.

Stark, Rodney. *What Americans Really Believe.* Waco: Baylor
          University Press, 2008.

Stevens, David E. "Daniel 10 and the Notion of Territorial Spirits."
          Bibliotheca Sacra 157: 628 (October–December 2000):
          410–31.

Thomas, Robert L. *Revelation 1—7: An Exegetical Commentary.* Chicago: Moody Press, 1992.

_____. *Revelation 8—22: An Exegetical Commentary.* Chicago: Moody Press, 1992.

Tuschling, R. M. M. *Angels & Orthodoxy: A Study in Their Development in Syria and Palestine from the Qumran Texts to Ephrem the Syrian.* Tübingen: Mohr Siebeck, 2007.

Unger, Merrill F. *Biblical Demonology: A Study of Spiritual Forces at Work Today.* Reprint ed. Grand Rapids: Kregel, 1994.

_____. *Demons in the World Today.* Wheaton, IL: Tyndale House, 1971.

Walvoord, John F. *Daniel: The Key to Prophetic Revelation.* Chicago: Moody Press, 1971.

_____. *Jesus Christ Our Lord.* Chicago: Moody Press, 1969.

_____. *Major Bible Prophecies.* Grand Rapids: Zondervan, 1991.

West, Robert H. "Milton's Angelological Heresies." *Journal of the History of Ideas* 14:1 (January 1953): 116–23.

Williams, Arnold. "Milton and the Book of Enoch: An Alternative Hypothesis." *Harvard Theological Review* 33:4 (October 1940): 291–99.

Williams, David. *Deformed Discourse: The Function of the Monster in Medieval Thought and Literature.* Montreal: McGill-Queens University Press, 1996.

Wolpe, David. "Angels in Jewish Tradition." BeliefNet.com. http://www.beliefnet.com/Faiths/Judaism/2002/04/Angels-In-Jewish-Tradition.aspx.

About the Authors

H. Wayne House is Distinguished Research Professor of Theology, Law, and Culture at Faith Evangelical Seminary in Tacoma, Washington, and an Adjunct Professor of Biblical Studies and Apologetics at Veritas Evangelical Seminary. Formerly he was Associate Professor of Systematic Theology at Dallas Theological Seminary and Professor of Theology and Culture at Trinity Graduate School, Trinity International University, and Professor of Law at Trinity Law School. He has a JD from Regent University School of Law, a ThD from Concordia Seminary, St. Louis, an MA in Patristic Greek from Abilene Christian University, a ThM and MDiv from Western Seminary, and a BA in Classical and Hellenistic Greek from Hardin-Simmons University.

He has been author, coauthor, and editor of over thirty books, author of more than seventy journal and magazine publications, and a contributor to several books, dictionaries, and encyclopedias. Among his many books are *The Nelson Study Bible* (NT editor); *The Battle for God*; *Charts on Open Theism and Orthodoxy*; *Charts of World Religions*; *Charts of Christian Theology and Doctrine*; *Chronological and Background Charts of the New Testament*; *Charts of Cults, Sects, and Religious Movements*; *A Christian View of Law*; *Restoring the Constitution*; *The Jesus Who Never Lived*; *Israel: The Land and the People*; *God's Message: Your Sermon*; and *Intelligent Design 101*.

Dr. House serves on the board of numerous organizations and served as president of the Evangelical Theological Society (1991). He leads study tours to Israel every year, and on alternate years to Jordan and Egypt, and Turkey and Greece. He has been married to Leta Frances McConnell for forty-three years and they have two grown children, Carrie and Nathan, and five grandchildren. He may be contacted at info@christianstudytours.com for interest in travel to biblical lands. His website is www.hwhouse.com.

Timothy J. Demy has authored and edited more than two dozen books on the Bible, theology, and current issues. He has also contributed to numerous journals, Bible handbooks, study Bibles, and theological encyclopedias. A professor of military ethics at the US Naval War College, he served more than twenty-seven years as a military chaplain in a variety of assignments afloat and ashore with the US Navy, US Marine Corps, and US Coast Guard. He has published and spoken nationally and internationally on issues of war and peace and the role of religion in international relations. He also serves as an adjunct professor of theology at Baptist Bible Seminary.

In addition to his theological training, which he received at Dallas Theological Seminary (ThM, ThD), he received the MSt in international relations from the University of Cambridge and MA and PhD degrees from Salve Regina University, where he wrote about C. S. Lewis. He also earned graduate degrees in European history and in national security and strategic studies and was the President's Honor Graduate from the US Naval War College. He is a member of numerous professional organizations, including the Evangelical Theological Society, the Society of Biblical Literature, and is Fellow of the Royal Society of Arts (UK). He and his wife, Lyn, have been married thirty-three years.